PALACES IN THE SKY
a year among Tibetans

ted reynolds

GODWIT

To Iain and Aileen,
the world's leading grandchildren

Published by Godwit Publishing Limited
15 Rawene Road, P.O. Box 34-683
Birkenhead, Auckland, New Zealand

First published 1997

© 1997 Ted Reynolds

ISBN 0 86962 000 3

Cover design by Mirella Monteiro
Cover photographs by Ted Reynolds
Typesetting by Kate Greenaway

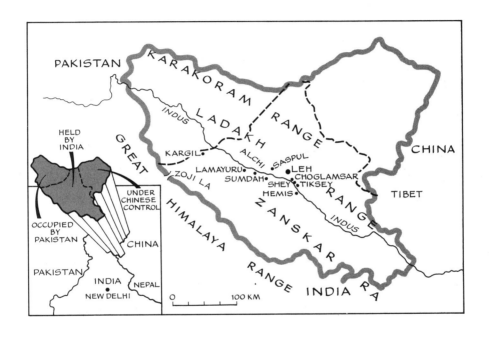

one

Tomorrow we are going to ambush the prime minister. At 10.30 she is due to land at our little sloping airfield that lies pinched between two mountain ranges. From there she will be driven up to the polo ground to tell people to vote for her in the election, then it's straight back to the plane.

She must be the most powerful woman in the world and she is hated as much as she is worshipped. Yet the army has made virtually no security arrangements — not even one motorbike outrider and nobody to guard her from the rear.

Her best chance of protection will come from the fat, purple-faced man who will sit on her right: Sheikh Abdullah, chief minister of Jammu and Kashmir state, and one of her steadiest long-term enemies. We guess he will be wearing his general's uniform, so his rig-out may include a shiny leather holster and a revolver that he could fire at an attacker.

In the front seat will sit an aide-de-camp decked out in military uniform, gold cord and tassels. But armed? Almost certainly not. At his side will be a sergeant driver from the Northern Army. Definitely unarmed.

Northern Army troops who can be spared from their endless and pointless skirmishing war with China are being sent up and down the valley to herd voters from distant villages and bring them to the polo ground on the trays of army trucks. Some troops from the Ladakhi Rangers will be at the polo ground, not really to protect the prime minister, more

7

to keep a pathway open for her car. Men of the Indo-Tibetan Border Police could have been called in for guard duty. But they are far away and out of sight patrolling icefields and uninhabited valleys.

Not that we plan to kill the prime minister, for goodness' sake. But our ambush will be unlawful. So we have been enquiring about security. It pays to know.

Between the airfield and the polo ground the land is mainly desert. Unable to conceal ourselves there, we are planning to advertise our presence in a way that will make us look like just another pack of fawning admirers and therefore completely ignorable. This morning, to mark our ambush point, we sent the camp truck and the camp carpenters to span the roadway with an arch that now holds a sign aloft: 'Well-Come Madame'.

Tomorrow all the men teachers except me are to stand in front of the arch. Because I have frizzy, mouse-coloured hair, freckles and blue eyes and therefore, up here in Central Asia, look like some outlandish wog, I have been handed the dirty job. Out of sight behind the arch I shall have to try to keep two truckloads of Tibetan children standing in an orderly manner for half an hour. And I am to give the signal for a spontaneous shout of welcome when the other men have released Madame.

Everyone assumes, without question, that I want to take part. And I don't mind. Usually I am an orderly little office worker — suit, silk tie, umbrella — in a South Pacific seaport. So it makes a change, dressed rough against the cold, to be waylaying Mrs Ghandi three and a half kilometres above sea level.

I guess, though, that our efforts will be a waste. If we have all this energy and organising ability — not to mention the contacts to tell us the prime minister's movements and her feeble security arrangements — we would be better off putting the same effort into finding food. Famine grows worse by the day, and I have learned to dread the visits of Karma, the man who doles out our vile and tiny rations.

Damn it, damn it. And damn everything. Here he comes now, bringing the galvanised buckets from which he serves the pig swill that we are now reduced to. At least there's no ladle sticking up from either bucket. So that's a sign that the meal is likely to be one potato each. Again.

On bad days a ladle in the buckets means that lunch will be a grey, moist material, a sort of cold gruel made, I think, from crushed barley that has been boiled for several hours. I tried it once. When we have potatoes, the cooks toss them unscrubbed and uninspected into cauldrons and when the potatoes grow soft enough to eat they are tipped into buckets, which the house mothers lug off to their children. Karma delivers to the adults.

He is in his forties and has a big grin and crinkly eyes. Three front upper teeth are missing. His earrings are speckled turquoise the size of pigeons' eggs. Each stone is threaded with string and each string passes through his pierced lobes. His wife, who is called Yeshi Bum, tied the strings and is proud of Karma and his earrings. When they are standing together she often moves one of his lobes forward to check that the knots are looking secure.

Apart from the lamas, Karma is the only man in the camp who still wears Tibetan dress every day. When I first came here he announced that he was my yok-po. Yok-po? I looked it up in the dictionary. Butler. My room is six paces by three. So I don't take much butling.

By now we have developed a routine. He comes to my door to show me what's in the buckets. I pull a face and either take something or shake my head. He giggles and carries on.

To Yeshi Bum I am an embarrassing idiot but, out of politeness, she tries valiantly not to laugh. As they walk around the corner and approach my door, she is already trying not to look at the doorway and see me there. But I have opened the door: already I am on show. An expression of horror and fascination comes over her face. She grasps her lips and tries to pinch them so tightly together that laughter cannot break loose. But it is hopeless and the laughter escapes. It sounds like barking and when she hears it she turns and runs. Karma gives me a don't-mind-the-wife look.

9

I choose a potato. Parts of it are still all right. I nibble around the rotten bits. What I can't eat I chuck out to the camp dogs. They rush the stuff. This is a refugee camp in the western Himalayas. The road has been snowed in for six months. We are nearly out of food. For breakfast the cooks manage slimy-skinned barley dumplings. After our one-potato lunch comes a bite of supper: leftover dumplings cut up into bits to look more bountiful. Things are on the point of improving, though, because fresh food must start arriving soon. It all depends on Zoji La.

One and a half day's drive away, Zoji La is the first and lowest pass on the road in. The passes are between 3000 and 4000 metres high and Zoji La, which is the first to stop the winds that were born in the Bay of Bengal, collects all the snow that falls when the air is forced up the wall of the mountains.

Well, it collects nearly all the snow. Here inside the ranges we get light scatterings. Yesterday, melting patches lay down by the Indus, which here is just a pup of a river that you can wade across. This morning a Shetland shawl of snow surrounded the queen's palace over on the other side of the river. This afternoon the snow is retreating further uphill. Above the palace the village of Stok has turned from white to brown — sure sign of a thaw.

So snow must be melting on Zoji La too, and when it does the trucks will get through again and there will be rice in the bazaar — a choice of rice even — and apples and eggfruit and tomatoes and new potatoes and those little white-yolked eggs from Kashmir. Then, as the hot season advances, the ultimate luxury will arrive: mangoes to eat while sitting on a sun-warmed rock and contemplating the stern beauty of our mountain desert.

Yesterday a rumour arrived that the snow on Zoji La has melted enough for army bulldozers to start pushing the rest of it off the road. Already, says the rumour, the first person of the season has managed to get in. The details are so unbelievable that the story is likely to be true.

The man is said to be a barefoot Dutchman who took the bus from Srinagar to Sonamarg. There he scrounged an old sack and cut it into strips. These he wound around his feet, lashing them down with bits of string. Thus prepared, the Dutchman began his climb up Zoji La. The snow was over his knees before he was quarter of the way up. But he made it. His feet, though, were in bad shape by the time he moved down the other side and into that desolate valley where Gujar nomads graze their flocks in summer. The valley is ringed with a lifetime supply of peaks to climb and its floor is without shelter. On the road in, this is the first place where you feel you are at last entering Central Asia. Through the valley the Dutchman walked, down Wolf's Leap Gorge and into Kargil, where he lay up while his feet healed.

Kargil is our frontier town, the final outpost of the Muslim world. Posters of the Ayatollah Khomeini still plaster the walls of shops and houses. In the streets a visitor walks a gauntlet of disapproving eyes. Kargil is also the resting place of washed-up remnants of ancient migrations. On the outskirts stands a village where doorposts carry those little tubes that mark Jewish households. The people speak a private language and the generations pass on a message that once, until they forgot the rites and prayers, their religion used to be different from anyone else's.

Up a side valley lies a string of hamlets inhabited by another race. Once a year they unite in a free-for-all sex festival. Anthropologists explain that this is to prevent the inbreeding that would otherwise weaken these tiny communities. But perhaps the people have not consulted anthropologists and just do it for fun. Now that a road runs past the valley, young German women try to visit the festival because they believe it is the world's last source of pure Aryan semen.

Kargil is also the first place where visitors see Tibetan faces. And quickly, after leaving Kargil, travellers cross a frontier of the heart. Islam fades. The Tibetan form of Buddhism takes over. The first Buddha appears, carved into the face of a roadside rock.

Kargil lies near the edge of dryness. From here on, years pass with virtually no rain and little snow. So from Kargil, the road remains open year round, which allowed the barefoot Dutchman to hitch a ride on a truck that was going to Leh, the little mud-brick capital city where today he must be a welcome sight: a hobbling sign that food and springtime will soon be on their way. And not only food. Bedbug powder will also arrive. Other adults in the camp have already selected me as the person who will buy and apply the powder.

The camp, about six kilometres upriver from Leh, is for the children — and, increasingly, for the grandchildren — of Tibetans who fled into India when China took over Tibet. I am a volunteer worker teaching maths, the only foreign teacher who has ever stuck it out, and because I am a foreigner I have been given a room in a unique building. It is the only one in the camp that has no prayer flags at each corner. So it carries no protection against evil spirits and Tibetans refuse to use it. Occasionally they report seeing a witch sitting on the parapet.

I have never seen her. But I do have troubled sleep. Bedbugs join me at night. I fear going to bed. The sting of a bedbug is sharp enough when fresh but it grows more maddening over the following weeks, and every night I add more bites to my collection. Everybody agrees on the best brand of bedbug powder and by now I have promised that in return for being shown how to use it I will also apply it to everyone else's cell.

And it is important that I must agree to do it for the others. They are Buddhists and therefore forbidden to kill — bedbugs or anything. Otherwise, as punishment after they die, they will be reincarnated as yaks or rats and their souls will have to spend centuries in animals' bodies before being born inside a human body again. But I have no religion. So I am free to kill, under their instructions.

This morning we are skipping school. Instead, the children gather near my cell where a pipe comes out of the ground and runs with water, even on minus-forty-degree days.

Since early winter the children have been allowed to go unwashed. No wonder. We have no hot water and the weather has been so cold that in

January and February people were wearing from three to six pairs of longjohns and woollen singlets under their outer layers. We all smelt the same, so no one noticed. But today we are all having a clean-up in honour of the prime minister.

Squatting on the concrete platform outside my window, the children pass around lolly-pink soap and wash their faces, torsos and arms, then share damp bits of towelling and do what they can to dry off. While wind and sun do the final drying, they turn their clothes inside out and send their fingertips on patrol along the seams, lifting with pincered fingernails the winter build-up of fleas and dropping the creatures near my front door.

When the children are washed and their clothing de-fleaed, we are all ready for Mrs Gandhi. The truck that yesterday carried timber for her arch of honour is running relays of us to wait for her at our ambush

The big clean up: children waiting for their first wash of the year.

point. Halfway into Leh the truck passes the mast of our local All-India Radio station. All-Indira, people call it, because of the time it devotes to reporting her doings. A sign beside the road announces that it is forbidden to take photographs of the mast.

On the airport side of the archway, the other men teachers stand together. They plan to commit a crime worse than photographing the mast. They will stop the prime minister's car and hand in a petition asking her to tell the Chinese government to withdraw its troops from Tibet. This will be an illegal act, because Tibetan refugees from Chinese rule are allowed to live in India only if they lay off political demonstrations. But they know this is meaningless. Forcing one Tibetan refugee to return to the control of the Chinese would set off an uproar about punishing people for being victims.

On the town side of the archway three hundred children line the road to call greetings to Mrs Gandhi once she has been given the petition. I am in sole charge of them.

Yesterday word of our plans reached the secret police. So a solitary Hindu is standing by the road when we arrive. Among dust and rocks his appearance of forlorn respectability advertises his sad calling: a suit that has given up hope of ever looking spruce again, an unwashed shirt, a weary tie. I line the children alongside the road and when they are in place, girls on one side, boys on the other, the secret policeman comes and looks at me, turns and goes downhill to the arch.

From his gestures I can work out that he is asking, 'Who's the foreigner?'

The Tibetans turn and shrug. 'Him? He's okay. He's just the maths teacher.'

The secret policeman moves to a patch of higher ground within range of me. I suppose he has a revolver under his jacket.

I walk up and down the road saying teacherish things.

'Stand straight. She'll be here soon.'

'No talking there.'

'You two, you're too close together.'

'Come on, everybody. You've got to be spaced out evenly.'

'That boy there, don't you dare throw stones at the girls.'

This is meaningless reflex talk that invites the children to ignore me. At morning assembly yesterday they listened indulgently to instructions on how they were to place themselves along the roadside: eyes right, right arms out, fingers extended to touch the neighbour's left shoulder, then stand easy while waiting but snap to attention when her car reaches the archway.

By now they can see that all this planning was born in that dreamworld that people in authority inhabit. Her plane has not yet appeared among the mountains. So why line the empty road now? There will be time to get organised when she lands. The children's minds turn down the volume control on my nagging until they can no longer hear me and are therefore free to go exploring. The girls walk away arm in arm, talking and laughing. The boys fight over whose turn it is to crawl through a concrete culvert pipe below the road. They throw stones at girls. They run into the gully beside the boundary of Leh hospital and collect plaster casts that nurses have tossed over the fence when fractured arms and legs have mended.

I stand stupidly beside the road, too proud to walk downhill and ask other teachers to shout the kids back into line. And I blame myself. If only I had been relaxed and silent and unfussy, the children might still be in their places. Because of my ineffectualness, Mrs Gandhi's heart will never be touched by the sight of cheering children. Tibet will remain in chains.

I look at the secret policeman. He could at least be human and grin contemptuously to show he has noticed my incompetence. Or I could send him a smile to show we both know life is made up of pointlessness and humiliation. But we just stare blankly, partly because I am growing wary of him. And he, perhaps he is jumpy at the thought that if I make a suspicious move he may have to shoot me without also killing Mrs Gandhi by mistake.

To break the gridlock of our stare, I walk over to the one child who has remained at her post. She is in VIA, my favourite class. A big, plain, lumpish girl, she is going through a disfiguring phase. She has a skin disease that she treats by daubing her face with a persistent purple liquid. Gentian violet? On bad days she hides the purple blotches of medicine by draping a scarf over her brow, behind her head and back again over her nose, leaving only her eyes visible. Dawa Metok is her name. Cruelly, it means Moon Flower.

I am undecided whether I like her. She is painfully keen to please, which means that either she is a born teachers' pet or that she is developing a crush on me. Not that it matters much either way, except that compliant children are a bore and fond pupils a danger. The rebellious and contemptuous are the interesting ones.

But here we are, Dawa Metok and I, together in the desert being watched by the secret policeman and ignored by the other teachers. So we stand together and find that we have nothing to say. Anyway, there is no need to say anything because the sound of the prime minister's plane now fills the silence.

Along the ridge behind Leh it flies, over the Red Monastery on top of the hill and over the abandoned royal palace below the monastery. Then the plane banks and falls in a plunging line down a side valley toward the Indus. Just when it looks as if it must crash into the mountains on the far side of the river, it swings in a tight arc as if tethered to another monastery, this one on top of a natural pyramid near the airport. And now, falling faster, the plane flies back up towards Leh, lands on the upward-sloping tarmac and performs the shuddering roar of a jet plane that has to stop very, very suddenly.

Hearing the sound of the screaming jets, the wandering children rearrange themselves alongside the road and look at me in a companionable and calming way: There, there, you needn't have worried, here we are again perfectly organised for Mrs G.

But one boy discovers that if he stands at attention, puts on an expression of surprised innocence and kicks at the ground, stones will fly

16

and splatter girls lined up on the opposite side. Instantly all the other boys take up his discovery. The girls cringe or hiss. I patrol a truce-line along the centre of the road, imposing peace in front of me and limiting the warfare astern.

Perfect peace arrives when an open jeep approaches from the airport. It is piled high with New Delhi reporters unaccustomed to altitude or cold. The sting in the air shrivels their faces and draws a veil of pale purple across milk-chocolate skin. The children stare in silence at them. The reporters stare uncomprehendingly at the nudity of our tilted desert, nothing but dust and rock and mountains in air of absolute purity.

Then comes a glittering maroon Ambassador car.

Down at the archway the other teachers spread themselves across the road. They sway as they bow. From the way they are carrying their elbows, they must be pressing their palms together in front of themselves. The car stops. People inside must be winding windows down to shout at the teachers and tell them to get the hell out of it because, now, to left and to right, the teachers are taking advantage of open windows and are poking their heads inside.

All, except the president of our local branch of the Young Tibet League, are dressed in Tibetan gowns. The president — clasping a scroll inscribed with the petition — is rigged out as an aged bar-room squadron leader: navy-blue double-breasted reefer jacket, grey trousers, blue shirt, silk cravat. The gowned men pull back from the car and the president hands in the scroll. The car shoots ahead.

Now comes my moment in the history of the world. 'Chik nye sum,' I shout, waving my arms like a conductor. 'Tashi delek!' One two three. Greetings! On cue the children join in, shouting 'Tashi delek!'

Inside the car I catch sight of the imperial nose and the trademark streak of white hair among black. Behind the car the other teachers are sprinting. We all join them. But my sea-level lungs are not built for running at this altitude and I lag. Beside me, also slowing, is Dawa Metok.

Mrs Gandhi must be a dab hand at giving a rousing five-minute speech because as Dawa Metok and I enter Leh I see the pyramid of reporters perched on the jeep, all heading back to the airport. Dawa Metok and I stop and find that we are beside a cake stall. Food in the midst of famine! I buy four cakes and give her two.

Beyond the shining smile of her thanks I see a familiar face in the crowd on the far side of the road. It is the camp discipline master, whose job it is to thrash children in front of morning assembly. So that other children can see the thrashings clearly, he performs his work up on top of a concrete platform. He, too, has seen Dawa Metok and me, and he rushes towards us, sudden rage on his face. Even as he runs, his right fist rises and swings backwards, ready to punch. His eyes are aimed at Dawa Metok's face.

This is my moment of challenge. And I know that I am going to fail it. I am a child of the 1930s and of the *Boys' Own Annual*. So I know that to protect Dawa Metok, young Carstairs in the annual would have stood in front of her and, with an elegant straight right, would have felled the evil, slit-eyed, little yellow man.

But I am also the child of today and people have impressed upon me the need for cultural sensitivity. It is part of Tibetan culture to bash kids and to keep on bashing until the children have forgotten what they are being bashed for. And I am the Tibetans' guest. They are letting me share their lives. I asked to come. They did not invite me to be their reformer and to teach them not to bash.

But the moment of challenge fails to arrive. Mrs Gandhi's maroon Ambassador is returning to the airport, now flanked by jogging soldiers who are clearing a way through the crowd, and as Dawa Metok and I brace ourselves for the discipline master's attack, he is brushed by a running lance-corporal.

Caught off balance, he stumbles and falls. I step forward and help him up. The impulse of rage is broken. He stares at us both. Confusion is overpowering his hunger to strike. It is an expression I have seen in the eyes of bulls that have just been shot through the head and who sense that they will die before they can kill their attacker. Then he shouts at Dawa Metok and turns away.

'What did he say?' I ask.

'Eating in street is forbidden.'

'What's he going to do to you?'

Sobbing stops her from answering.

two

Next morning I wake and start worrying about Dawa Metok. Will she be punished at assembly?

Only two teachers regularly attend the first part of morning assembly. The sportsmaster goes to make sure the children look devout during their prayer chanting. At first, as with some of Bach's plainer pieces, the chants sound like dull drones. Then, as you begin to know them, every performance unfolds new pleasures.

But before the chanting can begin, four rostered children must sweep the school quad, which lies inside a U-shaped range of single-storeyed mud-brick classrooms. The sweepers finish their job by making a pile of dust and paper just outside the quad. If any of the camp's sheep come by before mid-afternoon they will nuzzle out the scraps of paper and eat them. Otherwise the three o'clock dust storm, which will make every building invisible at twenty paces, will blow the dust and paper back into the quad for tomorrow's sweepers.

But today, now that the quad is swept, the children line up in classes in front of the concrete block on which the discipline master does his work. Standing on the block, the sportsmaster shouts 'Eye-ees right!' and, with arms outstretched and feet shuffling, the children click through the military routine of spacing themselves evenly over the quad. Up on the block, two children take the sportsmaster's place and start chanting.

Each morning I get the same gasp of pleasure. At the very moment

All lined up and ready to chant — and perhaps
to be thrashed.

that the first sound comes out of the leaders' mouths the entire school —
without the help of a conductor's beat, without even having been told the
names of the day's chants — starts to soar in unison. Minutes later the
chant will run into a silent pause or will flick from a deep humming to a
quick, fluttering soprano run of dee-dee-dee-dee-dee-dee-dee, and every
time each voice will crash into silence or switch from low to high at the
same instant.

As I gloat over my luck at being up here in the mountains listening to
them, I look for Dawa Metok to see if there is fear in her face. Normally
I would not endanger a child by sending a look of recognition. But today
feels safe. Usually, during chanting, the sportsmaster arms himself with a

21

bundle of thongs, each of which, for greater sting, is knotted at the end. And normally he patrols the quad, stalking children who show insufficient piety or let their attention stray. Even turning a head to see if he is creeping up behind brings punishment. The knotted thongs fly high and hit the face that is failing to look ahead. A gasp or whimper brings a second blow. Today, though, the sportsmaster keeps his cat in his pocket. He leans against the door jamb of the staff common room and talks to the boy inside.

The boy, Thubke Chophal, is, like Dawa Metok, in VIA. And he is a puzzle to me.

Most VIA children are teetering along the line between the pretend-world of children's play and the storms and yearnings of adolescence. Thubke Chophal, though, has slipped straight into middle age. He seems to have no friends among the other children and, instead of behaving as if teachers inhabited a distant and unknowable world, he is relaxed and joky in their presence and talks to them in the shorthand monosyllables of intimacy.

More than that, the teachers know his name. As far as I can work out the teachers treat all other children as interchangeable units that need no names. When I was new here, I made a map of each classroom and at each mapped desk wrote the name of the child who sat there. This seemed natural and obvious. To the other teachers, though, it was a fascinating novelty. Why did I do it? The question was like being asked why I breathe or how I manage to stand upright. So, instead of answering, I wondered why they asked. But one teacher needed no explanation from me. Her eyes brightened with comprehension and approval. 'How clever,' she said. 'Now you can correct them by name', as if such personal identification would bring unbearable shame.

The teachers have made Thubke Chophal their tea monitor, a job that keeps him further apart from his fellow pupils. While they chant he cleans the teachers' cups for mid-morning break, he carries water to the common room and he mixes milk powder or opens tins of condensed milk. Halfway through the morning's first lesson he will stand and walk out of the classroom to light the kerosene stove in the teachers' common room and stand by it while the water boils. He will do the same at lunchtime and for afternoon tea so that, three times a day, he cuts lessons short and misses the start of others.

Other children who want to leave the room stand, press their palms together and give a bob before launching themselves into the old formula: 'Please, sir . . .' So, when I was still feeling my way through Tibetan manners and the school's own style, I must have looked affronted when Thubke Chophal first sauntered out without asking permission. My face may have gone taut but the class's own lack of concern signalled that Thubke Chophal possessed special exemptions.

One day when we have biscuits at morning tea, I ask Thubke Chophal why we are having them. He gives no reply, which makes me worry more about him. Can no one else see that making him tea monitor is tossing aside his chance of getting an education? Or am I so unadaptable that, even here in a wilderness lost to the world, I continue to believe that students must be diligent otherwise how will they grow up to be scientists, office managers, engineers, doctors, accountants, lawyers?

In class nothing seems to be getting into Thubke Chophal's head. He is not surly, he is not disruptive. He is just passive and unresponding. When he gives no answer about the biscuits I realise what ought to have been obvious: he has no English.

Until last year Hindi was the language for all lessons. This year the school switched to English. There were good reasons. Tibetan exiles have set up their own communities all over India. In Calcutta and Madras and Bombay — and a thousand other places — Hindi is a foreign language. But English is India's glue, essential for children who will spend their lives scattered around the country waiting for the slow tides of history to turn and suck the Chinese out of Tibet.

I know my worrying shows how out of touch with reality I am. Look at the fruitstall at the camp gates. It is owned by a Kashmiri family. The husband works in the Jammu and Kashmir State Police, the wife is busy with babies and housework, so their eldest daughter runs the stall. She is seven or eight. And she is a model business woman, welcoming and cheerful, quick and accurate with change. She and I trade in a mixture of Tibetan, Hindi, Urdu, English and mime. She has never been to school and never will go.

I come from the privileged white world that insists on using and controlling the riches of the globe. By the fruit stall girl's standards the poorest of us are rich. We can afford to believe a decent education is a right. When we worry about the future of boys such as Thubke Chophal we are only indulging in the pointless luxury of being high-minded and of having charitable thoughts but no intention of doing anything: when I am finished with my work here I shall go home and will join in hogging the world's wealth. I shall, for example, burn petrol without thought, and in doing so, will help to ensure that my own children get all the chances while Thubke Chophal and the fruitstall girl get none.

The biscuits, I discover, are to celebrate the news that the Dalai Lama's junior tutor has been reincarnated, down the valley at Khalse.

The sportsmaster is still leaning against the door jamb with his back to the children, so I catch Dawa Metok's eye and raise an eyebrow. She sends back a look that I think means she dreads what may happen when the discipline master arrives, which must be soon because the other teachers are now beginning to appear. The women wear long gowns that are cut like perfectly severe dressing-gowns. From their waists hang the aprons that are a mark of respectability. These are woven on narrow backstrap looms as finely and tightly as the owner can afford. With every few throws of the shuttle the colour of the thread changes, and the apron is assembled by sewing three strips together with the rows of colours in the central strip out of alignment with the outer strips.

The men, though, wear cast-off clothes from Europe. The refugee camp is linked with charities in Austria, Belgium and Holland, which send bales of old clothing, but only for men and boys. Girls and women must keep to traditional clothing. So the men teachers arrive in T-shirts decorated with words I am required to explain: St Tropez. Wanna Nookie? Carlings Black Label. Over the T-shirts the men wear business suits that spent their youth in office blocks in Salzburg and Liege.

Morning assembly is always an open-air function. It never rains, the camp hall is too far away to use, the early morning sun is warmer than the classrooms will ever be until summer arrives. So Thubke Chophal brings wooden seats out from the staffroom on to the platform that faces the sun. We teachers sit and smile and gossip and store up warmth while we run our eyes over the chanting children.

As the chanting nears its end the discipline master enters the open end of the quad. He walks to the rear of the row of VIA children and paces his way along the row, touching the shoulders of the children he has selected for punishment. Dawa Metok is not among them. Today they are all boys.

But these are not boys who were brought up on the *Boys' Own Annual*; they have never read that decent chaps take their beatings in manly silence. When the discipline master touches them, they crumple at the knees, they throw up their hands, they wobble, they cry out in fear. Slowly the discipline master herds four boys before him and watches as they climb the punishment block.

Unwaveringly the chanting moves to its end and, when silence comes, the discipline master recites the boys' crime. Yesterday during morning playtime they climbed the stone wall that marks the upper boundary of the school grounds. Then, slinking behind rocks, they escaped into the boulder wilderness that lies between the refugee camp and Sabu village. There they hid, avoiding the rest of the morning's schoolwork.

How, he ask the assembly, could any Tibetan child be so ungrateful? How could any pupil reject the loving care of the Holy One? Far away in

Dharmsala His Holiness the Dalai Lama works to ensure the education of the pupils so that, when Tibet is free again, an educated core of young adults can restore the homeland to its sacred and ancient ways. But these four boys have spurned the Holy One's gift. If they cannot appreciate His Holiness's work for their welfare, then appreciation must be beaten into them. And let this thrashing be a lesson to any others who are ever tempted to slacken in their work for His Holiness's restoration as rightful ruler.

Here the discipline master stops, turns and walks into the staffroom, where the punishment strap hangs on a nail behind the door. It is his habit to coil the strap into a disc before striking children and when the boys see him emerge rolling the strap up tightly they launch themselves into the Tibetan way of showing remorse and abasement. They stick out their tongues and lower their heads. Repeatedly they throw their hands up to the crowns of their heads and drag curled fingers forward over the skull as if desperate to haul their hair down over their eyes.

The discipline master lunges for a boy, grabs his collar and pulls his pants down in front of the school. Now the minutes stop. On and on goes the beating. The other three boys have abandoned their head-scratching, have withdrawn their tongues. They stand in a huddle. One has stuffed his fingers in his mouth. All are slumped and weeping. Methodically the discipline master assaults each child. Teachers and pupils watch, their faces set in a display of blankness: neither encouragement nor disgust.

By the time he is finished the discipline master seems too weakened to return the strap to its nail. He stands unsteadily, with a fine wisp of foam just showing where the lips meet. The assembly stares at him; he stares out over the massed faces. Then he summons strength, dismisses them, turns and takes his strap back.

He is a small man. An earring made of a giant lump of turquoise has dragged the lobe of his right ear down to his jawline. The task of being discipline master is an extra that he volunteered for. His real job is to teach Tibetan culture.

three

Sunday today. No school. So I walk into Leh to post a daughter's birthday present.

A month ago I could have skated down the Indus to the airport and then walked up to Leh over the shingle fan that spreads below the town. But skating is off today because the Indus is flowing again, though only in the middle. Broad ledges of ice a metre thick and high above today's water level still cling to the riverbanks. Full flow will not return until midsummer, when unbroken months of rainless heat melt the edges of the glaciers at the head of every side valley and bring water chittering over rocks and into the river. Another sign of spring: willow bark is losing its shrunken look and is beginning to plump out and develop a sheen.

In Leh the shops have food again and the first of summer's traders — Kashmiris and Tibetans — have arrived from the Vale of Kashmir, riding on the backs of trucks and lolling against the bundles of goods they have brought. The Kashmiris rent empty shops for the season and are treated with suspicion: so smiley and so smooth. The Tibetans, though, have no veneer and no shops. They simply spread their goods on either side of the street that runs from the post office down to the creek where, at dawn, the town butchers slaughter sheep.

In theory, Ladakhis and Tibetans eat no meat. They are Buddhists to the bone and are supposed to be vegetarian because they are forbidden to take life. But the religion industry knows how to keep the letter of the

Chortens (left foreground) line the way up to
Tiksey Monastery.

law. So, as with bedbugs, the killing of sheep is done by proxy, and Buddhists are able to argue: Look, the animal has died already. Wouldn't it be a shame to let its flesh go to waste?

The killers are Muslims and just when the sun is lifting itself out of Tibet they lead the day's selection of sheep down to the riverbed boulders. The animals pause trustingly at the slaughtering ground when the men stop there and, like trained dogs, move forward to receive the knife when summoned by their killers. The butchers kick slithery bits of unsaleable guts into the creek, dump flesh and useful innards into willow baskets, lay the fresh sheepskin on top and crown the lot with the animal's head. On their backs they carry the baskets up to the main bazaar and into open stalls, where they suspend blobs of flesh from hooks that hang from the ceiling.

When summer comes, each day's supply of meat will develop black crusts of flies and I shall become vegetarian. Today, though, I watch the hunched butchers humping their baskets up from the creek and wonder whether I can work up enough enthusiasm to buy meat. But I cannot watch the butchers and their burdens for long because a young woman has stopped in front of me.

Her head is shyly lowered. Her lips, though, are smiling and her eyes are lifted upwards to look at me so that below the pupils shine two inviting half-moons of white: a pretty mixture of reticence and challenge. Then I recognise her. Dawa Metok. I switch from man to teacher. What is that child doing in town? Has she written permission? Why is she not back at the camp helping with Sunday's sweeping, washing, mending, weeding? And what about her homework?

I hear my own voice saying stiffly, 'Tashi delek, Dawa Metok', and wait for her to explain what she is doing in town.

'You are shopping, sir?' she asks and, grasshopper-brained, I am diverted from being her inquisitor and instead allow her to take the lead: 'No, I'm just posting this parcel.'

She takes it from me and giggles as she turns it over in her hands. Damn the girl, why does she titter? Has she never seen a parcel before? It has taken me a week's vigilance and prying to find wrapping paper. Nobody seems to sell it, and every scrap of paper is put through three or four uses before being given to the sheep to eat. It was only yesterday I found a fairly fresh sheet in the camp office and scrounged it from the sportsmaster's wife.

Dawa Metok returns the parcel to me. 'Post office is not accepting,' she announces.

I let a raised eyebrow reply — 'We'll see about that, my girl'. Then I head for the post office, Dawa Metok beside me.

'And how much for this one?' I ask the man behind the counter.

He lifts the parcel with distaste as if I were asking him to smell a stale urine sample. He reads the address. He tests the knots. He is amused by the deft but futile labour that has gone into folding the paper and tucking in the corners. He returns it to me. 'It is not being possible,' he says.

I stand my ground.

He summons the postmaster.

The postmaster is a man of experience. He has seen parcels like this before. At a glance he comprehends its faults and announces the prescription for an acceptable parcel: calico cover, sewn seams, sealing wax along the seams.

'Sealing wax?'

'Of course, sir. Otherwise naughty mans will trifle.'

Dawa Metok takes command. She leads me to a fabric stall and tactfully stands back to let me mime my requirements. I pay the first price the stallkeeper asks and ignore her shocked intake of breath. One rupee poorer but a quarter of a metre of calico richer, I stand on the footpath and look helpless. What next?

'Now the tailor,' says Dawa Metok, and in no time the cross-legged man is zapping his needle around the seams.

This time Dawa Metok warns me of an oversight — 'You did not make price,' — and when she watches me hand over yet another rupee and decline to take the offcuts she rebukes me: 'Oh, my God, such spending, such spending.'

But I don't mind. All I want now is sealing wax. But she does not know who sells it. And I can hardly blame her. Shopping in Leh can be a puzzle. It took me months to work out which hardware shop sells butter (sewn up in a bag of yak skin) and I have only just discovered that if you go into the shop that has a display case full of condoms on its frontage you can be sure of finding tins of tuna inside. But who would stock sealing wax?

I get an inspiration. Why not try the newsagent at the Tibetan end of the bazaar? He is affronted when I ask whether he stocks sealing wax. The question hints at lax management and he replies in a hurt tone. 'Of course. How many sticks?' To make up for my rude questioning I buy half a dozen. This is a lifetime's supply. Dawa Metok draws in another sucking hiss.

As we prepare to hunker down on the footpath — she to hold the parcel, me to light matches and drop circles of red wax along the seams — I spy, on a street vendor's tray, a collection of old steel seals and decide that rich blobs of sealing wax stamped with my own Tibetan signet will give a sense of extra grandeur to the calico parcel. The seals are five rupees each — less than a dollar — and I buy the first that does not bear the good-luck mark that in Tibetan is called yung dung but in Sanskrit is known as svastika.

Soon Dawa Metok and I are admiring the excellence of our workmanship. She imitates the squeaky Hindu postmaster: 'Now no naughty mans will trifle.'

When I laugh she ducks her head and grins up at me. Again the shrinking coyness. Again the challenging eyes.

This time the man behind the post office counter accepts the parcel without a flicker, put stamps on it and commands, 'Please to present at guichet.' I run guichet through my computer and get a mental printout: 'French for ticket-window, now obsolete in English.' While this process is going on, Dawa Metok, driven to distraction by my carelessness, issues an offended order to the man behind the counter: 'Cancelling all stamps!'

The man looks at her and bangs his date stamp over the parcel. She takes it and checks to see that each postage stamp has been smeared with ink, thus thwarting the naughty mans in the Indian Post Office who prise off unfranked stamps and sell them again for their own profit.

She leads me outside to the tiny barred window on the street frontage, where she raps for attention and raps and raps again. As we wait snowflakes appear, spaced well apart, idly twirling and melting where they land. Behind the iron bars across the guichet, a miniature door opens inward. Dawa Metok lifts the parcel to signal our need. A grumping noise comes from behind the door. A hand unclicks the grille and swings it open. Now two hands appear. Between them peeps the face of the man who directed us to present the parcel at the guichet.

His hands withdraw the parcel. The grille clicks shut. The guichet door closes. Snow falls. Dawa Metok and I look at each other in triumph. We have posted a parcel.

'Drink tea at my house,' says Dawa Metok.

'Your house? But you live at the camp.'

She gives no answer. I walk beside her. Our backs are towards Tibet, our faces towards Pakistan. Straight in front of us, perched on a rock above the bazaar, rises the nine-storeyed palace where King Senge Namgyal — the name means Victorious Lion — used to rest between wars.

If you measure kingliness by battles and dead bodies, Senge Namgyal, who died in 1640 aged around seventy, was the greatest king of Ladakh. Today's Ladakh is only a scrap of the area where he slaughtered and ruled. Now it is powerless, absorbed into India and classified as one of India's most backward regions.

India. On the map it looks like a nursing bitch's dug hanging low from the belly of Asia. But along the belly-line a second part of India rises northward, a triangle pricking into Central Asia. This triangle, in which Dawa Metok and I live, is disputed territory. Pakistan governs some by right of conquest. China claims profitless glaciers in the high northern reaches; India garrisons its Northern Army in Ladakh to defend the same perpetual ice that China wants. And Muslim Indians down in the Vale of Kashmir bicker, bomb and kidnap to force India to give Kashmir to Pakistan. In return, Indian troops kill, jail and torture the northern Muslims.

On the ground in Ladakh you immediately notice cruelly expensive military posturing: all summer, great convoys carry diesel, firewood, mule fodder, guns, shells, armoured vehicles, food and rum. Military encampments impose ramshackle ugliness on a landscape that Ladakhis once enhanced with giant monasteries that appear to grow naturally out of the mountains they bestride. On the surface, country life is unchanged. Warplanes rip the air but, below them, farmers using methods known to Christ and Chaucer tend barley fields that look like baize cutouts stuck to dun deserts.

In villages, though, and in Leh and in valleys popular with trekking companies, the military road means change. Visitors with fashionable notions about preserving other people's ancient hardships wince at the sight of Ladakhis adopting new comforts. Look at them! Instead of sticking to dung fires they have switched to cooking on Indian copies of 1930s primus stoves. They are even putting kerosene lamps in their houses.

But the life that is being changed was set by previous invaders. When the great Tibetan empire spread from Burma to the foothills of K2 in Pakistan, Ladakh absorbed the language of the conqueror. Eventually, long after the Tibetan empire had shrivelled and left Ladakh independent, the Tibetan branch of Buddhism undermined Ladakh's survival. In their vast palace overlooking Leh the descendants of the Victorious Lion immersed themselves so deeply in pious rites and chanting that they could not be bothered with the business of government. Instead they appointed a dynasty of hereditary prime ministers to do their work.

Out in the countryside, the abbots in their monasteries became the effective rulers of their districts. Power had descended on them without design. The monasteries had become moneylenders and ended up controlling the souls and the earnings of an awed and indebted peasantry. The abbots also developed the ultimate old-boy network. They believed they had acquired such spiritual merit that they could decide their next incarnation and, naturally, they chose to be reborn as their comfortable selves. When an abbot died, a newborn boy was proclaimed to possess his soul and, like some queen bee, the boy was nurtured inside the monastery until old enough to take over the abbotcy.

Sunk in piety, the kingdom spent its spunk. The great posts of state were assigned in the cradle. Idiocy and indolence were no bar. Raw merit was sentenced to life at the end of a mattock. For a time few great harms followed: we ordinary people are already governed by necessity and are too considerate to let our masters ever see how little their commands are needed. But, in the end, the enclosed and drifting kingdom wallowed into crisis. A descendant of Genghis Khan came raiding and the king of Ladakh sent a fatal request to his distant neighbour, the Maharajah of Kashmir: Please come and save us.

Send help he did and, in return, required annual tribute to be paid. The kingdom became a vassal, but such a slack vassal that it defaulted on its payments. The maharajah, then the dominant force in northern India, sent an army of 10,000 to collect the rent. Accustomed to victory, the 10,000 faced a scratch team of 5000 raggle-taggle barley farmers led by an eighteen-year-old boy and armed with bows and arrows to fire at the maharajah's riflemen. The maharajah's army stripped palaces and monasteries and sent its master a caravan of 170 horses burdened with gold, silver and Central Asian silk rugs.

Still the silly king could not see that he had lost his kingdom. Again he failed to pay tribute. Again the maharajah's army returned. This time a governor was installed, the king was bundled out of his palace and sent to a lesser palace in Stok and told to stay there — the same palace, now inhabited by a descendant's widow, that I was watching weeks ago when spring was lifting the last snow from field, village and hillside.

Dawa Metok guides me up through a knot of twisted streets, through a rubbish dump and then up to Senge Namgyal's palace. Violently she begins kicking at its carved front door. The door is chained shut and, during a pause in her kicking, I peep through a hole and see on the inner side a padlock clamping two links of chain together. Someone must be inside.

She resumes her kicking. The hinges are so loose, the door so huge and heavy and the chain so slack that the door wobbles and I grow afraid it will fall and I shall be blamed: another foreign vandal wrecking our heritage.

No one comes and Dawa Metok's anger rises. She says, 'Damn that boy', and looks at me to see whether I have registered her command of idiom.

I climb the crag on which the palace stands and find a ruined window. Inside — but too far down to jump — lies a heap of rubble that must have come loose from the inside of a wall. I call 'Julay, julay, julay!' This is the first word people learn in Ladakhi. It means hello and is also used as a noise of agreement to encourage a speaker to keep talking. No response comes but Dawa Metok beckons me to come down to her — beckons with palm towards the ground because our upward-palm beckoning is a signal so rude that people have been too embarrassed to explain what it signifies.

From behind the door comes the rattling of the chain and the sound of a great baulk of timber being lifted. The royal door opens. A boy monk stands in front of us.

He and Dawa Metok ignore each other in a way that suggests long familiarity. So he concentrates on me. 'Go now,' he commands and makes a shooing movement.

I pull out a five-rupee note, smooth it on my palm, turn it over, fold it and put it back in my pocket. Avidly the boy monk watches each movement. So I pull it out again and give it to him. Dawa Metok and I enter. Immediately she takes command, leading the way through the gloom.

Moving into the palace is like entering the ruins of an opera house that has one forty-watt bulb burning in the auditorium and lightening the gloom just enough to let the eyes catch the hint of the ragged edges of collapsed floors rising in tiers above us. Aloft in the gods, sunlight leaks through cracks in walls. Ahead, around a twist in a passage, glows a dull hint of light. Cautiously we follow the passage and we are in the king's chapel. A gilded Buddha several storeys high stands in front of us. Around his feet flicker butter-lamps.

The boy monk melts into the darkness and returns with ritual instruments of worship, which he tries to make me buy. When he sees I am uninterested, he produces a great hat of the same cut as a cardinal's except that this one is black and the lower side of the brim is covered with fur. To fire my greed, he flourishes the hat and then, with sudden force, pulls it on to his own head. Dawa Metok and I hear the screech of fabric ripping when the brim comes apart from the crown. Unconcerned, the boy monk struts like a grandee, flaunting the wreckage of the hat.

Gradually, as the eyes adjust, the details of the chapel grow distinct. A few columns remain, bearing gilding and paint. Each area of separate colour is outlined by a fine raised border. But other columns have collapsed and the entire trunks of poplar trees have been rushed into place to prop up the ceiling.

Dawa Metok interrupts my inspection: 'Please follow.'

I half hope she is going to lead me out — where's that cup of tea she was offering? But, no. She walks ahead to an outer wall from which stone steps jut. She leads the way and I, who have a lively dread of heights, follow her up and up and then along passageway tunnels where floors shiver underfoot as she guides me to yet more flights of stairs. Sometimes she points warningly to gaps in floors or mimes the way I must be careful to climb without letting my feet touch some particularly suspect step. How does she know these details when she is supposed to be living out at the refugee camp?

The light increases and presently we step out on to a flat roof. On it stands a loggia where kings and courtiers could sit blotting up warmth during the eighty winter minutes when the sun has a chance to heat the air. The loggia faces the early afternoon sun and its three walls break the upriver wind.

As a demonstration of sumptuous living in this untimbered land, there is also a summer apartment, its walls constructed of Kashmiri-style carved latticework to let air but not sunlight in. The panels must have arrived on the backs of horses led and cajoled for the fifteen-day walk from the Vale of Kashmir.

Elsewhere, walls of plastered mud bricks are painted with scenes advertising royal bravery in the hunt, plus one section that, surely not intentionally, displays diluted courage. At its focus point a tethered tiger, looking wonderfully defiant, strains to get at a man armed with a spear. The man stands just outside the radius of the tiger's chain, balanced for a lunge at the animal.

Dawa Metok and I start to grin because somewhere below us we can hear a wandering voice: 'Go now. Go now.'

'Those are his only English,' she says. 'He is my small brother.'

'This is my house,' says Dawa Metok.

We have collected the boy monk. We have watched him checking that all the butter-lamps are full. We have waited outside the palace door while he rearranged the chains and clicked the padlock shut on the outside. We have picked our way down the path from the palace. And now we are together in a stone-walled yard that has a low, one-roomed building in one corner.

The building, which stands on the wasteland that is being used as a rubbish dump between the palace and the town, looks as if it was built as stabling. The yard has room for three or four horses and inside the building there is room enough for four horses to sleep. The floor is of beaten mud. Bedding is at one end. At the other end are pots, some china bowls, a kerosene cooker made of brass and the inevitable vacuum flask from China, covered with pictures of roses. From it Dawa Metok pours tea. She insists that I sit on their bedding while they sit cross-legged on the floor. The boy monk and I are not introduced.

'My mother, she is dead last year,' says Dawa Metok. 'My father is at ITBP' — this is the Indo-Tibetan Border Police camp between the refugee camp and Leh — 'and this boy, he is burning butter for the queen. I am living here when I am not schooling.'

four

Lobsang Tensing is in charge of the refugee camp, a monk in his fifties, not tall, getting fat. The Dalai Lama's sister is said to dismiss him as indecisive and has sent Jigme Kunga here to act as the sort of assistant who can produce action.

We are all in awe of Jigme Kunga. He and Lobsang Tensing are a match in opposites — slow, smiling, unruffled Lobsang Tensing, stately in movement, seeming to trust everybody.

In his wake darts Jigme Kunga, slight, nervy and as quick and alert as a minnow. Talk around the camp is that when Jigme Kunga was a lama he put himself through extraordinary rigours of study — marathon readings of holy texts, then the traditional staged attacks in which shouting students and teachers try to destroy one another's arguments — but that as soon as he had achieved high academic honours he chucked away the maroon and yellow gown of priesthood and married instead.

Looking at his wife, whose grace and smile make me feel like melting, I imagine myself being happy with her. But when Jigme Kunga (respectfully, we all call him Kunga-la) visits on his own to help me drink rum, he sighs, stares away and talks of happy days with books and learned disputation.

Politically the two men seem shrewd operators. If the general of the Northern Army is reposted, Lobsang Tensing holds a farewell party. An hour of quickfire rounds of rum is followed by a gobbling contest as nuns pass plates of rice and chilli-hot cubes of sheep liver. Then as decisively as if a guillotine had fallen the party is over and invitations are being sent out for a party to welcome the next general. Civil bigwigs get the same treatment.

This is not bribery. It is respect. It is hospitality. It is grease for wheels. It makes for trouble-free dealings when our foreign enclave must do business with our host country, to which Tibetans are an occasional and mild irritant but are also a steady cause of tension and rancour with China.

Parties are, in addition, a setting to study Lobsang Tensing and Kunga-la. Always Lobsang Tensing seems assured that arrangements are going well. Empty glasses will be refilled in time; everyone will behave; the nuns will serve food promptly and amply. So he gives himself over to enjoying his guests.

Kunga-la, though, is tense. He sees an empty glass; he semaphores the

Lobsang Tensing (centre) concentrates on one of the gambling tables
at the school picnic.

man who is holding the bottle, he searches for the man who is supposed to be carrying the jug of water.

He looks at his watch. Are the nuns on time with their cooking? He peeps into the kitchen, is blown backwards by an explosion of nunnish resentment at being spied on.

Kunga-la looks around. No, of course Lobsang Tensing has not noticed his assistant's humiliation: he is too busy laughing or listening. But I have been watching, and Kunga-la sends a shrug and a wry grin to say this is the price of being dutiful, this is the cost of protecting the boss from his own slackness.

Well, Lobsang Tensing is a ditherer. But he doesn't get into tizzies. His face is wrinkle-free except for laughter lines. I imagine he does not know how to yell. He does, though, know disappointment, and recent disappointment at that. He is just back from France, where he called on charities to make sure they remembered the needs of the camp children.

That was the easy bit. The disappointing part was French food. Lobsang Tensing is a giggler and now, safely back home, his face puckers with revulsion and then he laughs in disbelief when describing the food he saw in France. He giggles at French people's amazement when he told them he was homesick for his usual food.

At Leh and in little roadside teastalls the favourite food is a sort of ravioli served in broth. It is called moh-moh. In good times moh-moh has minced meat inside. During our winter famine, you could sometimes find a bowl of moh-moh in town but, instead of meat, the ravioli was wrapped around scraps of onion. The other standard meal is tuk-pah: same broth as moh-moh plus flat noodles and scraps of unidentifiable parts from the insides of sheep and goats.

The pasta is always homemade. Every teastall has its own pasta machine, and the people here boast that they taught Marco Polo how to mix flour and eggs together to make noodles and how to turn sheets of pasta into ravioli. Remembering this, Lobsang Tensing discovered the secret of survival in France: go to Italian restaurants, order naked noodles or ravioli and a bowl of consommé, dunk the food in the soup and dine — such a simple solution, so why had the French not discovered it for themselves?

A year ago, when I wrote to Lobsang Tensing asking if he needed an unpaid worker for twelve months, he wrote back: 'Yes. Come. And bring something to break stones.'

I had visited the refugee camp years before during a walking holiday, so I knew how hard the refugees had worked to get it established. They had been granted the use of some land between Sabu village and the Indus, and on it they started building and planting.

The land is a shingle fan: a triangle of rubble that floods have washed out of Sabu Valley. The fan widens as it nears the river. The surface is covered with coffin-sized boulders. Under them lie sand and gravel. Every morning before breakfast, each child had to fill a box of stones and dump them outside the camp boundary, and all day the adults either attacked boulders with sledgehammers or tried to make barley grow in sand. For every kilo they sowed, they harvested 500 grams.

Work and water changed everything. Up near the head of the shingle fan they found underground water, and with terrible labour, the men and women wrenched boulders and shovelled sand until they had a trench a kilometre or more long and deep enough to be below the reach of freezing temperatures. On my first visit, during that walking holiday, I was taken uphill to see the trench. It was so deep that the workers were out of sight. From a distance only the shovel blades were visible, jerking up from the trench to toss shingle and sand away.

Since then a European charity has sent water pipes. So today we have water on tap, and in the courtyard of every children's home the children grow cabbages and a few flowers: cosmos and sunflowers.

When I arrived this time, carrying my own sledgehammer, I expected to be shown a year's supply of rocks and told to break them. Instead Lobsang Tensing and Jigme Kunga met me at Leh and both got the giggles when I handed over the sledgehammer. Why the giggles? Had they been hoping for a pneumatic hammer instead? Or, when Lobsang Tensing told me to bring something to break stones, was it a test to see if I would be too scared to come? Not that it matters now.

They put me straight on to teaching maths, plus giving me a junior class for general science and the most senior class for English. Why maths? From early childhood I had been assured I had no head for sums but now, every morning, I stand in front of the VIA pupils, and, with easy confidence, lay bare the secrets of mathematics.

How do I manage, especially as the lessons are far in advance of anything I did at school? Easy. As I could have done as a boy, I sit up every night to teach myself tomorrow's lesson from the textbook the children are using. My nightly preparation usually costs two candles, a cheap price for confidence in the classroom. And all that mental exercise is affecting my mind. Numbers are hacking pathways through the brain. Sometimes I find myself looking at a problem and coming up with an instant answer, without knowing how I got it.

I am sure, though, that one VIA boy knows I am only just keeping one step ahead of the class.

Sonam Dakpa is small, with a fine-cut face. Most of the children are from western Tibet, the wild west of an already wild country. The area most of them come from is called Jhun Thang, meaning western plain. It is far higher than the land we are on and must be one of the least hospitable places on earth.

The boys — though never the girls — are full of stories they have heard from fathers and grandfathers about the glorious life to be led there: nomadic summers spent guiding herds of yak from pasture to pasture across limitless and empty land; great trading journeys in autumn, driving beasts laden with summer's surplus butter and with salt and soda scraped from the beds of the lakes that formed and then disappeared when the great island of India collided with the sweet, warm coastline of Central Asia and pushed orange groves and harvest fields up into the Himalayan sky.

The recent ancestors of VIA used to plod from Jhun Thang to the distant splendours of Lhasa and even over the mountains to Nepal to sell and buy. Because Jhun Thang is too bitter to grow grain, the men had dispensation on their return home to slaughter surplus yaks once the temperature was low enough to keep the flesh deep-frozen through winters of ease, of feasts and drinking and baby-making inside the black yak-hair tents.

These western people have rough and jolly faces to match the life, and among them Sonam Dakpa looks a foreigner. The others have dark brown faces overlaid with apple-red skin on the cheeks. Their eyes are slitted against dust storms and snow glare. Their lips are broad. They like body contact: they shove and elbow one another when on the move, huddle together like newborn pups when still.

Sonam Dakpa is the colour of old ivory. He is reserved and remote, and he observes the ways of the others as if he were some boy emperor seeing simple people for the first time. Where the others are promiscuous in their friendships, he makes friends with only one other boy, and that boy has the same pale skin and the same metropolitan polish.

When I stand in front of the blackboard, the other children listen attentively, scowling with the effort of absorbing the ideas I am trying to put across. But Sonam Dakpa has a mind like a hungry trout. In one dash it gulps down the day's lesson. Then his brain retreats to still water, where it can easily keep station, waiting in case any fresh fact comes drifting by.

Whenever I stumble in a lesson or try an explanation that is in danger of turning illogical, Sonam Dakpa's body tenses and his head lifts itself a fraction as if he has seen the trap I have placed in my way. When I notice these signs of extra attention, I imagine he is taking a connoisseur's pleasure in seeing whether I am quick-witted enough to join him in spotting the peril I have created and whether I shall find some way around it.

I admire and pity Sonam Dakpa. How does he stay awake through my lessons when he needs only two minutes to digest the facts that the others take half an hour to turn over and examine? How can I give him the attention and the shove that he needs to reach his potential?

I can't. I am on the boundary of my own knowledge and can take him no further until I have spent another night of swot. And, anyway, the crowded classroom is so small that some of the fifty children in it are able to hide all day. Little Rigpa Dorjee, for example, comes up to the waist of some boys. Squashed between muscular dunces in the back row, he goes for days without being noticed or helped. He is just on the borderline between making it and falling into the discard heap. So he needs help, too. And gets none.

But Sonam Dakpa worries me most. His disengagement, his superiority, his boredom — these are danger signals. Sooner or later, another teacher will resent his cleverness, will turn nasty and try to thump him into servility.

The boy whose future I do not worry about is Karma Yeshi. He is the class conboy. So carefully has he cultivated servility that he has turned flattery and elaborate politeness into the weapon with which he controls teachers. He is already at work on me and has insisted that I must be his special guest when he is established in Lhasa as the prime minister of a new and free Tibet. He promises me that he will make sure I have as much tuk-pah as I can eat. At this, I make a grave show of courtesy and accept his invitation.

Karma Yeshi flies into tooth-flashing ecstasy. 'Thank you, thank you, sir. My people will be very pleased to see you and to thank you for your work for Tibet. And my cooks will make the best tuk-pah in the world.'

Karma Yeshi is shortish and thickset. His upper teeth seem to be all canines, triangular, coming down to a point. So his smile, which is quick, frequent and large, carries hints of menace. He is also eleven-fingered, so he is a chu-chik.

Chu-chik — meaning ten-one — is the Tibetan word for eleven and is also the word for any eleven-fingered person. So far I have noticed two eleven-fingered people here, which is two more than I can remember seeing over the past fifty-three years. It cannot be freakish to have seen two in such a short time; there can only be a special word for eleven-fingered people

44

Karma Yeshi, the conboy of VIA, and — or so he says
— the future prime minister of Tibet.

because there are enough eleven-fingered people around to need it.

Karma Yeshi delights in completing a problem in maths. Or does he merely delight in making a show? In any event, he throws the class into disruption when he completes an exercise.

The classroom is divided by an aisle that has rows of six desks on either side. Everything is jammed so tight that the desks touch their neighbours and the chairs are hard up against the desks in the row behind. Karma Yeshi sits up against a wall and, when he gets his answer to each morning's set of problems, he jumps up on to his chair, kicks at classmates to make them inch their buttocks forward and create a pathway along the chairs. Now he scrambles along, using other children's heads and shoulders as props until he reaches the aisle.

Here he turns himself into a priest's assistant. In a solemn procession of one, he opens his exercise book in front of himself and holds it facing me as if it were some holy text resting upon a lectern. Now, in solemn paces, he advances on me, bows, elevates the book to make it easier for me to see and announces: 'I have the answer, sir.'

If I say his answer is correct he beams, his dog-teeth flash, his face glistens with happiness and he turns to the class to announce his triumph. If I say his answer is wrong he tries to persuade me I am wilfully discouraging his efforts, and sets out to explain each logical step that produced his answer. Along the way he sees where his reasoning went screwy. Unabashed, he now sets an even beamier smile across his face and tells me that I am the very best teacher he has ever met.

I try a wan smile in return to show that I appreciate his performance and can see right through it.

Privately, though, I am astounded. Karma Yeshi cannot yet be thirteen. But already he has learned that no praise, no matter how transparently self-interested, can ever be too rank or too gross for human consumption. His thick and confident application of flattery has won him a special exemption from the school's rules for keeping the sexes apart.

I learned this one afternoon after school when I was walking down a lane between the children's houses. The courtyard walls stood about two metres tall and on top of one of them sat Karma Yeshi.

'Welcome to House Number Ten,' he called down. 'You are visiting us, I hope, sir.'

'No. I'm in a hurry to get over to the monastery library.'

'But, sir,' said Karma Yeshi, 'the house mother will be sorry. You cannot walk by without coming inside.'

Karma Yeshi launched himself into the air, landed in front of me and gave a smile that said he knew he was a bullshit artist — and a brilliant one. 'Please, sir,' he said.

So I followed him through the gate in the wall. House Ten was one of the older homes so it lacked the solar heating being built into the newest. Instead it had a conservatory-style entrance hall, so warm that, even with dusk approaching, the children had shed bits of their outer clothing. They sat cross-legged, doing their homework on a dazzling timber floor. When I exclaimed at the shine, the children showed me how they had achieved it: floor polishing was their sport. They jumped on to polishing rags lying against the wall and, standing on them, started a skating race. Then the biggest girls dumped the smallest children on to the rags, grabbed their ankles and held chariot races.

Looking angry at being upstaged, Karma Yeshi told me I must inspect the storeroom. He marched me to a door and shoved it open. 'Storeroom, sir.' Inside were piled twenty trunks of galvanised iron, each painted with a child's name.

'Boy's room, sir,' announced Karma Yeshi, as he pushed open another door. The room was as clean and bare as only institutions can be, except for ten bunks around the walls, with bedding tucked in precisely. The girls' room was the same, formidably tidy, no private possessions.

'Now, sir, see staffroom.' He opened another door. Inside I saw a woman sitting on a narrow bed and fingering a rosary. 'House mother, sir,' he explained. Then, in English, he told her: 'Ronner-la is inspecting.' 'Ronner' is the best Tibetan tongues can manage with my surname and 'la' is an honorific to flatter the powerful and ancient.

Karma Yeshi led me out through the courtyard, where two patches of cultivated ground were showing young sprouts. 'Cabbages, sir,' said Karma Yeshi pointing to one patch, and 'Sunflowers, sir,' as he pointed to the other.

With much gravity I shook his hand and thanked him for an interesting visit. He squirmed with pleasure — or was it simple triumph in having created and taken charge of a little pageant?

'Karma Yeshi,' I told him, 'you really are a fraud, aren't you?'

'Why? What is that meaning?'

'Well, how come you're still in House Ten? And living with all those girls? You're old enough to be in the big boys' house by now, aren't you?'

The big boys' house stood well away outside the camp walls, and when boys were approaching sexual maturity they were sent into nightly exile in the distant all-male compound.

In a sudden storm of anger and fear Karma Yeshi replied, 'I am never going into boys' house. Their house mother is a witch. So I tell my own house mother I love her too much to go.'

Sly triumph replaced fear. 'And here I am staying.'

five

It often happens like this. I turn up at school and am the only person there. A Tibetan living in Europe might make a similar complaint: 'I arrived at the office on 25 December and the doors were locked.'

We have a marvellous lot of holidays to celebrate. Even though we talk of India as if it were some far and foreign country, we stop work for every passing Indian festival. And we also knock off for every Tibetan holiday: Saka Dawa, National Uprising Day, Zamling Chisang, the Dalai Lama's birthday, Choekhor Dhunchen.

But today feels different. Instead of having free-range children rushing around on a day off, the camp seems deserted. Then in the childless quad, I hear the formless hum of unceasing talk, the eruption of laughter and complaint. The noise is coming from the square outside the camp hall, where the senior school and even the kindergarten are being formed up in rows, all graded according to size, smallest children at the upstream end, the tallest at the end nearer Leh.

All the adults are in a fuss. The discipline master and the sportsmaster are taking sightings along the rows and looking as if they despair of getting the lines straight without a theodolite; other teachers are clasping hands or pointing at the sight of a wobbly child; house mothers push a child a little this way, then that, and are being yelled at by the discipline master.

Through the dust Lobsang Tensing approaches, a solid and calming presence in his yellow and maroon gown, one sleek shoulder exposed. He

49

is attended by Jigme Kunga, whose jumpiness dilutes the processional calm of Lobsang Tensing's entry.

Now Lobsang Tensing stands in front of the assembly and, in spite of all that effort to get everyone in line, spots someone whose presence disrupts the pattern: me. He bends sideways and whispers something to Jigme Kunga. In turn Jigme Kunga moves his head nearer the discipline master, points at me and passes the message on. Now Tsepon Lungshar summons Dorjee Gyaltsen, the music and dancing teacher.

Dorjee Gyaltsen has gone out of his way to make himself my friend. Shrunk by embarrassment, he walks over to me: 'Please, sorry, Ronner-la,

School outing: children file down from the Red
Monastery towards the outskirts of Leh.

50

but the director, he says this is only for Tibetans.' I move off with as much indifference as I can manage.

Hours pass. Alleys and open spaces are deserted. Underneath his calm, Lobsang Tensing is usually an urgent and disorded public speaker who, with rising excitement, repeats phrases and follows bypaths in the mind instead of ignoring them and sticking to the point. Sometimes I have seen him lose his way and need Jigme Kunga to prompt him back. Today his speech in the camp hall must be trapping him in a maze.

Even when the children are dismissed from the hall and camp life resumes, movement is withdrawn and limited. Adults will not talk of what happened after I was excluded.

So I sit by my window. On my desk I have Thackeray's *Vanity Fair*, borrowed from the Choglamsar Monastery library, where, among its shelves of religious texts, stands a glass-fronted bookcase full of all the books people are supposed to have read at school. I grow impatient with Thackeray — so much repetition — and impatient with camp life because I have been waiting too long this afternoon for the signal which will mean that if I care to perform my side of a ritual I shall be able to discover what went on at the meeting.

The ritual will go this way: Dorjee Gyaltsen will walk by, will turn his head towards my window and will give one of his fleeting, questioning smiles. Dorjee Gyaltsen is a great one for quick, unconfident smiles. He is also a desperately torn man, inescapably Tibetan but aching to be part of the world's mainstream. Sometimes he brings me ties he has collected from the charity ragbag and wants to know which one would look smartest in Bombay. But mainly he is obsessed by disco dancing and insists that he must introduce disco to the refugee camp, otherwise the place will become a backwater.

He asks me, 'Everywhere disco is very, very fashionable, yes?'

And I say yes because I have not the heart to tell him everyone has forgotten disco dancing.

Dorjee Gyaltsen is also torn in the way of every second-generation immigrant. Back in the 1960s his parents fled Tibet with their children and a string of little harsh-paced ponies and settled on the bed of boulders that the Indian government assigned to refugees coming into the Upper Indus. For a time the government provided them with food. But that could not last and, when hunger came, Tibetan herdsmen who knew nothing of cultivation could work up no enthusiasm for growing barley.

Dorjee Gyaltsen began hanging around army camps, looking for odd jobs that would bring in money for his family. Soldiers paid him to clean the flues of their heaters but one winter evening, when walking home upriver, he collapsed from cold and hunger. 'I am a little boy dying when peoples find me.'

A Tibetan man tells his rosary in the old people's
section at the refugee camp.

Bright at school, he was sent over the mountains to the teachers' training college at Dharamsala, where the Dalai Lama had established his court and his government-in-exile. Dorjee Gyaltsen had a girlfriend there and for a time wanted to marry her but in the end decided she was too modern. 'Always she is arguing. Always!'

So when he came back from training college he married Dolkar, who is content with the old ways. She is docile and obedient. They have a boy and a girl. And he has decided that two children is all they are going to have. So he has had Dolkar fitted with a contraceptive loop.

'That is very modern,' he tells me. There is delight on his face and, this time, no need for hesitation, no waiting for my endorsement. His parents disapprove, though. They want more and more grandchildren. But Dorjee Gyaltsen has made up his mind. Two are enough.

His parents are becoming a trial in other ways. The more modern he and his own family become — washing his body, brushing his hair, cleaning his teeth, wearing ties and cast-off business suits — the more outlandish his parents seem, grubby in homespun clothes they never wash, still stuck with the habits of living rough.

Down here, at 3500 metres above sea level and squeezed into a pinched valley, his father still maintains a string of ponies — eleven of them at last count — inside stone walls he built to house them. But now he has grown too feeble to work or travel. So he has no need of horses, has not really needed them since escaping the Chinese. But still he keeps them because a man, if he wants to be anyone, must own horses. Dorjee Gyaltsen's father has to buy fodder for them. So the horses eat and the parents go hungry. Dolkar has to walk up to the camp where the old people live and take them food.

Dorjee Gyaltsen himself is low in the camp pecking-order. Because he so hankers after Western things? Or because the other staff think little of the singing and dancing he teaches? I suspect he seeks my company so he can practise English, which he speaks with drive and daring, though he suspects his sentences are littered with laughable error. 'The other teachers, they despise,' he tells me.

Another reason he visits is that I have black-market rum.

As the days warm up, the convoys of army trucks that take two days to grind over the Great Himalayan Range, to skirt the Zanskar Range and to sidle around the outliers of the Karakoram Range, arrive laden with cases of rum marked 'For the Use of Indian Army Personnel Only'.

There are said to be three grades: officers, other ranks and mules. The other-ranks rum instantly goes on the black market, where I have three suppliers: the woman who runs the teastall over the road from the camp entrance, Jigme Kunga and the false rimpoche.

Seeing it is only a dollar a bottle, I said to Jigme Kunga, 'Why not sell me a dozen?' A dozen in one go! From the look on his face I began to feel I had made some lewd proposal. So I switched to the woman over the road. She seemed edgy, as if I might be a disguised policeman trying to trap her. And when I left with a bottle hidden in an inside jacket pocket she used to walk with me to the door and watch me in a worried way.

Then I heard of the false rimpoche, Tensing Sangpo.

A rimpoche is a spiritual master who has reached human perfection and is qualified to be reborn in Nirvana. But such is his lofty nature that every time he dies he chooses to come back as a person to help lesser souls into a good reincarnation. Tensing Sangpo believes he is the reincarnation of the last abbot of Spituk, the monastery atop the pyramid down by the airport. But the monks there laugh at him. Long ago they installed another reincarnation and are not going to change now.

Tensing Sangpo has bounced back from rejection and has established a new religious niche-market for himself. Learning of all the refugees now living up on the Ladakhi end of Jhun Thang — the western plain of Tibet — he has made himself into a sort of bishop to the people there. At the end of school terms, when children are trucked back to their parents, Tensing Sangpo hitches a ride to Jhun Thang and attends to his flock.

54

The job must pay well. He has married a strikingly beautiful nurse at the camp hospital, he has built the finest house in the camp and has fathered a boy who is recognised as a genuine rimpoche. These successes, though, have not raised his status in the camp. People stop to smile at the little rimpoche (he is still at kindergarten) but they hurry past the false rimpoche.

But not me. When I called at his house he was lying barefoot on a divan playing with his pet goat. A bottle of rum stood on the floor beside him and, not wishing to interrupt his own playtime, he pointed at the bottle, a spare glass and a glassful of water. It was the standard other-ranks rum. That is, it felt like liquid fishhooks. At high octane the choking it produced masked the flavour. Watered down, it revealed a mildly nauseating taste.

This was precisely the stuff I was expecting to buy from him but before we could get around to talking business the front door opened — Tibetans do not knock — and in came a spectacularly dirty and ragged little man, who scuttled towards the false rimpoche, fell on his knees and started making obeisance.

Tensing Sangpo, giving me a look that said 'Don't go away. This is shop but I won't be long', swung his legs on to the floor, walked to the corner and sat cross-legged. Now his visitor stood, turned, scuttled, knelt and resumed the obeisances, repeatedly lifting his hands high and throwing himself flat on the floor.

The false rimpoche sent me glances of boredom until the man crept closer to him and began whispering. Now Tensing Sangpo became pastor and friend, confidant and support. Both men held their heads close together. Entreaties drew a rumbling calming response from the false rimpoche. The soothed man put something in Tensing Sangpo's hand and he transferred the something to the pouch in his cloak.

Out walked the visitor. Up stood Tensing Sangpo. He made a little shuddery move, as if changing gear from bishop to slygrogger and sat beside me. 'I hear you want to buy rum.'

With much application, Dorjee Gyaltsen and I have trained ourselves to shudder down the army rum with water — and now, looking up from *Vanity Fair*, I see Dorjee Gyaltsen performing his afternoon rum-begging ritual.

At the pace of a Catholic priest sauntering in his garden and reading his breviary, Dorjee Gyaltsen passes my window. His head is down, his hands are behind his back. His gaze is steadily on the ground ahead. Then, when he has only just passed my door, he looks up, flicks his head backwards and experiments with a smile directed at my window.

I raise a hand so he can see it in the sunlight. Now Dorjee Gyaltsen's smile changes gear, shifting from diffidence to delight. He has been seen. He has been recognised. He has found someone who does not despise him, a friend whose rum bottle is never empty. And he is welcome. So I open the door. He is bubbling with the news the other teachers have been repressing.

One of the house mothers is pregnant and five boys have admitted — boasted? — that they could have been responsible. This is very evil news. He shakes his head and searches for a better word. It is much shaming.

I laugh at his solemnity. 'Come on, be honest. When you were a boy you would have paid money to get a house mother pregnant.'

He giggles. 'But this is different. She is having that baby from so many boys. She is shaming our director. She is shaming Tibet. She is shaming the Dalai Lama. The director said this.'

As punishment, Lobsang Tensing has expelled her. She has lost her home and her job. I ask where she will now live. Dorjee Gyaltsen shrugs. And how will she be able to feed and clothe the baby? He seems puzzled that I should ask. He begins to lose patience with me and repeats, as if I have missed the central point, 'She is shaming us all.'

Well, what about the randy five? What punishment for the boys? Dorjee Gyaltsen assures me they are also being punished. 'For many months they are having no pocket money. Each boy is fining five rupees.'

He glances down at his glass. It is empty. I reach out for my eight-rupees-a-bottle rum and pour him more.

He grins and lifts his glass with a sigh: 'A very shaming day.'

While Dorjee Gyaltsen and I are drinking, the door opens and in steps Karma Kesang. He is the office messenger and a bit of a misery-guts. He is twenty-three, is married to a camp tailoress, is under threat of being fired and dreads the future. And with good reason. If Jigme Kunga fires him, how will he be able to support his wife, and any babies that arrive, plus his divorced mother and his grandmother?

He once told me, 'When my parents were divorced, my father he was hating my mother.' His father gave his mother no money and she had trouble finding food for the family. They were then living in Dharamsala and his mother told Karma Kesang, 'If you love me, go to the orphanage at Choglamsar.'

So, eight years old, he travelled along the far side of the Himalayan foothills, caught the bus at Srinagar and came through the mountains to Leh. From there he walked up here to the refugee camp and asked to be brought up. Karma Kesang kept passing all his school exams and in the end the camp sent him back to be with his mother and to spend two years at high school there. By then he was qualified to go on to teachers' training college. The camp found him a place at the Madras training college, where it promised to maintain him. On graduating he would take up teaching at the camp school. Our camp also runs an old people's home, so before the long voyage south to Madras, Karma Kesang brought his mother and grandmother to Choglamsar to live and waited for them to settle in before going off to training college.

While he waited he fell in love. Jigme Kunga told him that he would ruin his career if he married before qualifying. As a teacher he would earn $64 a month and his wife would get $10 a month for her work. Together, their $74 a month would easily support his mother, his grandmother, his wife, himself and any children.

The pilgrim's way: an old Tibetan hobbles from
chorten to chorten to gain a good reincarnation.

Karma Kesang now sees that Jigme Kunga was right. 'But my cock
was bigger than my brain, don't you see.' So he married.

Jigme Kunga, who sometimes drops in for a rum, is still angry with
Karma Kesang — all that work and effort spent on him. And what for?
But he gave Karma Kesang work as office messenger. The job is worth
only $30 a month and is strictly temporary because it had already been
half-promised to a man with children to raise.

The reason Karma Kesang is now visiting me is that he is carrying an
invitation from Lobsang Tensing.

While Lobsang Tensing was telling the school about the shameful house mother and the five-rupee fines he was imposing on her young lovers, the office workers were busying themselves by typing grids of asterisks across and up and down sheets of writing paper. Inside each oblong of asterisks they typed invitations to a play in the camp hall. Then they snipped each sheet into asterisk-bordered rectangles and sent Karma Kesang to deliver one invitation to each of the director's special guests.

By the time Karma Kesang reaches me, only ninety minutes remain before the curtain rises. I mutter at delays and disorganisation. Karma Kesang remains on his feet, staring at the bottle. Dorjee Gyaltsen rocks uneasily, shifting from buttock to buttock, which signals to me that he, a trained teacher, would feel put out if he were to drink rum with the camp peon.

I rescue them both from desire and snobbery by turning on my gruff act. 'You jokers had better piss off. I've got to go out with bloody old Lobsang Tensing.'

Both look shocked: I really must remember how everyone venerates the director. But the words work. Both men disappear. I cook, eat, splash water over my face and hurry off.

Barred from the hall in the morning, I am now the guest of honour. The director and I bow and smile and, while everyone else sits cross-legged, he leads me to two chairs he has had placed in the best position. We sit and watch the curtains that have been drawn across the stage.

Two boys stand centre stage in front of the curtains, ready to run to the walls and haul the curtains with them. But from behind come whispered orders in Ladakhi: 'Wait! Wait!' The boys tense until a fresh command comes, now in English: 'Okay.' The boys trot to the walls. The curtains part. And there stand the Sabu Players.

Sabu is my favourite village, my dream home. By rights it is out of bounds to foreigners — too close to roving Chinese patrols — but on days off I like to climb to Sabu, to crouch beside the creek and watch fools' gold — or is it real? — twist and twinkle on its bed.

I search but never find the Sabu god-woman, who is supposed to hide bits of sheep and fowl guts in her hand. She then performs magic surgery on her patients, with her bare hands extracting rotten parts of their bodies and hurling the dying organs into an enamel bowl. Grateful patients press money into her hands. Shuddering under the force of the psychic powers she has unleashed, she accepts reluctantly — and posts the money to a daughter who is taking an MA course at the University of Kashmir.

Tonight, having picked their way through two kilometres of giant boulders, the Sabu Players have come to present the story of Senge Namgyal, the Victorious Lion.

So here is the king, alive again on our village stage, surrounded by his generals as they brag about how easily brave Ladakhis will march down the river and defeat the lowly and contemptible men of Baltistan. Safe in the king's palace, they show one another how, with knives and daggers, they will slit Balti throats and drive steel clean through Balti hearts. But, even as the heroes of Ladakh puff and boast, the Sabu Players slip into their second scene. From the side of the stage Balti warriors tiptoe with swords at the ready. The warriors gargle a war cry. Swords slice the air. In no time, the All-Victorious Lion of Ladakh is on his knees cringing and whining for mercy.

Now the scene cuts to a cell in the dungeons of the king of Baltistan's palace, where a princess has been given the job of delivering Senge Namgyal's food and drink. As she enters his cell with plate and pitcher she giggles a little, she backs away, she advances, she wiggles a hip. Senge Namgyal begins to circle her and put out hands to touch her. In one shameless gesture of immodesty, she throws her veil to the ground. The curtain boys rush to centre stage and we are saved from having to watch, before our very eyes, a replay of the house mother and the five boys.

Beside me, Lobsang Tensing rocks with pleasure. The hall hums with excitement. Adolescent boys slap one another in glee.

Next scene: King of Baltistan: Sir, are you the viper who has made my pure and innocent daughter pregnant?

King of Ladakh (smirking): Indeed, I am, sir.

King of Baltistan: You vile toad! Now to save her honour I must set you free, and you must take her home to be queen of Ladakh.

The final scene is a revel back home in Senge Namgyal's palace as he and his courtiers celebrate the triumph of cockiness over courage.

Chorus of hangers-on: Truly the Victorious Lion is supreme! With bold thrusts of his privy lance he planted the seeds of his triumphal homecoming! How we rejoice in the prowess of our great lord!

The two stagehands run the final curtain across. Lobsang Tensing's laughter is so out of control that he has to hold up his head with his hands. Some of the younger children laugh so much they fall over. The house mothers, except for the expelled woman, have thrown arms around one another to save themselves from crashing to the floor with mirth.

six

Something is going wrong. When I step into the classroom I see a special tension. Children keep sending sly glances to the left rear corner of the room. But, whatever the trouble is, they still put themselves through their antique ritual. They stand. They raise their hands to chest height, press their palms together, give me a bob and a ragged chant: 'Good mor-orning, sir.'

Poor creatures, now they must try to follow my explanation of negative numbers. I spent much of last night wondering why mathematicians ever had to dream up negative numbers. But suddenly, in front of the blackboard, it all comes to me and I can explain why: 'On Monday Dawa Metok lends Dorjee Namgyal five rupees. Now he owes her five rupees.' Heads swing left rear as the class turns to look at Dorjee Namgyal. Children titter — mockingly, I think.

He is the biggest boy in VIA and clearly adult. I don't especially enjoy having him in the class, but that must be my fault. He is the class hero, muscular and athletic, nimble, quick and driving on the basketball court and the easy winner in middle-distance running. He takes admiration calmly, works hard at lessons, is diffident with me.

His name, incidentally, has nothing to do with Senge Namgyal. Some Tibetans and Ladakhis are said to have family surnames that are kept secret. Otherwise the names by which they are known are descriptive and are given to them by lamas. Nor are their names necessarily permanent. If a child is sickly, the name may be blamed for being unlucky and the lama will select a new name to bring improved health. Dorjee means unyielding (it is also the word for a ritual religious object) and Namgyal is Lion.

In the back of the classroom the Unyielding Lion blushes, grins and ducks his head when the mention of his name produces head-swinging and tittering, and Dawa Metok, on hearing his name, jumps as if from an electric prod and throws her hands over her face.

I try to drive right through this interruption. 'So, Dorjee Namgyal, because Dawa Metok has lent you five rupees you owe her five rupees. You own nothing. You are in debt. If you had to make a quick note of what you are worth you could write it down like this . . .'

I find a stub of chalk and write on the blackboard -Rs5.

'That's negative five rupees. Then on Tuesday Dawa Metok lends you five more rupees and five on Wednesday, five more on Thursday and another five on Friday. By Friday night Dawa Metok has lent you all her money. She still owns it. She is worth twenty-five rupees. But what are you now worth? How could you make a note of what you are worth?'

I stare at forty-nine puzzled faces and one contemptuous face. It belongs to Sonam Dakpa, who has curled his lip and is looking straight through me. I look hard to him. He controls a tremor that is threatening to turn his sneer into a smile. I suspect — I am positive — that he knows the answer, that he probably foresaw the question. This time I get the feeling that he is no longer playing boy emperor but is sliding into the despair of boredom and is simply giving up.

Like an auctioneer, I examine faces and look for a gleam. No eye reveals that anyone has worked out an answer. So I turn to Dorjee Namgyal.

But he does not notice me. He is too busy talking to Dawa Metok. Both are looking pleased with themselves. His upper lip has moved into the tense smile of a man who is trying his luck and testing how far he can go. Dawa Metok is having another bad day with her skin infection and her cheeks glare with blotches of purple ointment. But his attention lights her face. She glows as mothers do when babies laugh after their bathtime.

63

'Dorjee Namgyal,' I say, and their lovers' tableau breaks apart as he and Dawa Metok lift their eyes to me, 'this lesson is about you. Say Dawa Metok had five rupees and lent them all to you . . .'

For twenty seconds I can go no farther. The class erupts with hoots and shouts. People turn to laugh at them both. Karma Yeshi has laughter tears on his cheekbones and he thrashes his thighs to control his laughter. Dawa Metok and Dorjee Namgyal freeze in embarrassment.

To keep myself in command I invent some stage business that will hide my own expression. Turning and bending, I open my desk drawer and pull out the first piece of paper that comes to hand. It is my old map of the classroom, showing where the children's class teacher told them to sit. It shows that Dawa Metok has not shifted from her place. But Dorjee Namgyal has slipped himself four places sideways so as to be close to Dawa Metok, one row behind her and one seat to the right of her so that if he leans forward and she backwards they are within easy whispering range and at an angle to each other so that they can look eye to eye without Dawa Metok's having to turn her head too much.

'Okay, kids, settle down.' Now I rush the words to give no time for another outbreak. 'On five days running Dawa Metok lends Dorjee Namgyal five rupees. Twenty-five rupees altogether.

'If Dorjee Namgyal wants to make a note of what he is worth he can write it down as negative twenty-five rupees. On Monday he is worth negative five, by Friday he is worth negative twenty-five. Five times negative five is negative twenty-five.

'So, negative five times five is negative twenty-five. Negative seven times three is negative twenty-one. Every time you multiply a positive number by a negative number the answer is a negative. Positive times negative is negative. Negative by positive is negative . . .'

Well, I think that's the proper reasoning. But my mind is on Dawa Metok and Dorjee Namgyal. The school has a terrible love of rules, and I guess that Dorjee Namgyal's sideways shift, especially to be near a girl, will bring trouble. Should I head if off? But half the rules are pointless. So

I decide the hell with it all. They are good pupils, quick enough to keep up with lessons and steady enough to handle the distractions of pleasure. I do nothing.

'Okay, kids. End of lesson. Thanks for listening.'

They all file out. Sonam Dakpa looks slumped. His eyes make contact with no one.

Dorjee Namgyal and Dawa Metok walk close together, leaning inwards, talking, laughing. She looks enchanted and confident. She must know all the other girls are wondering how, with all her purple splotches, she managed to get the class heart-throb.

I, too, am puzzled. But not at how she got him. Only at why everyone laughed when I talked about lending money.

Talking of negative and positive numbers, midwinter's minus forty degrees has now swung to forty degrees — that is, forty degrees hot. It doesn't feel anywhere near as exhausting as that temperature down on the plains because here there is almost no humidity. So sweat doesn't stick around. The skin feels comfortable. And shade is cool.

But it can be stinging heat. Move from shade into sunlight and the change comes as a blow. My winter walk to school, along the most direct line, now follows an elaborate path: a quick dash from my door and over to the willows that grow beside the overflow from the stand pipe, an easy stroll in their shade, then quickly across open ground until I can dawdle in the shade of the camp hospital, then a flickering quick-slow walk, quick in glare, slow in shadow.

If I am absent-minded and follow winter's unprotected path on the sunny side of a stone wall, my heat-pestered steps are watched by the black button eyes of grey lizards that lie imbibing heat on the stones, unmoving except for a rhythmic pulse that stirs the lime-green frills around their necks.

Because our invisible sweat is instantly sucked up by dry air, we cannot see our water loss, can only measure it by thirst. When Thubke Chophal makes his sticky-sweet tea — sugar, sweetened condensed milk and tea leaves all thrown into the pot together — we teachers drink four cups at a sitting. And still we wave empty cups in the air to signal that he must hurry over with the teapot for another refill.

What are the children doing for their own thirst? I do not know. The nearest water for them is the pipe near my door. But during school hours it is out of bounds. I suppose they have the sense to know that all they have to do is put up a hand — 'Please, sir, may I leave the room?' — and run invisibly behind the lizard-rich wall to get to the water.

The first class in the afternoon is a hard time for them and for me. In the comparative cool of the morning pupils who have decided they have already learned as much as they will ever need to know stare out our one window and track the passage of the few clouds we ever see as they sail the sky on voyages to Turkestan and Samarkand. But in the afternoon the heat by the window is so sapping that heads teeter forward, fall on desktops and stay there with eyes shut.

My four sexpot girls are the worst for inattention. In the morning they sit by the window, steaming with resentment and silently broadcasting their despair at being locked up in a schoolroom with a doddery old man when at least they deserve a frisky nineteen-year-old teacher in jeans and a T-shirt that asks: Wanna Nookie?

In the morning they build barricades of schoolbags and textbooks in front of themselves. Against these ramparts they prop up comics which, at four paces from me, they must believe I cannot see. When I take those four paces and ask them to put their comics away and their schoolbags back on the floor, I smell rebellion. But by early afternoon their resentment has been felled by heat and boredom, and I can see no gain in stirring them.

This afternoon, though, my neighbouring teacher, Kelsang Gyatso, kept the girls awake.

God knows, there must be reasons for me to like Kelsang Gyatso.

Often, on evenings when he is rostered to take the big boys for homework, he visits me on his way over to their hostel. And he accepts glasses of rum with no sign of reluctance. So he must mean to be sociable. But once he has a glass in his hand he merely sits on my bed staring at me in silence, his face set in misery. He will not share his thoughts. I cannot get on with marking children's work. I try to make conversation; he has no responses.

Now he has invited me to a picnic for two. It has been set down for today and for weeks I have been dreading the hours of mournful silence in his company. But at least it turns out to be a good day for a picnic. By early afternoon the temperature is painfully high and I savour the prospect of evening cool beside the adolescent Indus, relaxing and drinking the chang he has promised to bring.

But some time before two o'clock Kelsang Gyatso's punishment of four boys in his class destroys anticipation — not that he raises a hand against them: he forces them to torture themselves. He starts with shouting, of such violence that even the torpid girls by the window raise their heads. To the rest of the class he sounds so violent that automatically work stops and there is no point in trying to tell the children to settle down.

Our two classrooms are linked by a raised open-air platform that has a pipe rail running along its edge to save children wobbling off the platform and falling one and a half metres or more down into the quad. The pipe, though, was built too high to do its job properly. It might save wobbling adults but is so high that a child could easily fall straight underneath without a show of grasping it.

Unsteady with rage, Kelsang Gyatso grabs the pipe as he orders the four boys to hook their legs over it and hang upside-down like trapeze artists. Threatening worse punishment if they move, he returns to his classroom. In the heat they whimper, then groan.

We pretend to work again but after a full ten minutes the heat, the pain in their knees and their leg muscles have them openly crying and calling for mercy. Kelsang Gyatso comes out and threatens to kick the boys in the face if they do not shut up.

The headmaster, walking through the quad, stops for a look. 'What have they been doing, Kelsang Gyatso?'

'They were all asleep.'

The headmaster grins, nods and walks away. Kelsang Gyatso leaves his victims hanging and goes back into his classroom.

The boys resume their crying, now violently, and when Kelsang Gyatso comes running out one boy slips, falls on to the concrete and slides into the quad.

Now Kelsang Gyatso is beside himself. 'I'll teach you. I'll bloody teach

Rosary in one hand, prayerwheel in the other, an old
man accumulates merit for judgement day.

68

you. Down into the quad. All of you.'

The biggest boy, who had been able to ease his pain by taking some weight on his fingertips, slips down on to his palms, falls sideways and manages to stand to help the smaller boys down from the rail. Kelsang Gyatso takes out his prayer beads so he can keep a tally and orders the boys to perform one hundred standing squats. 'Okay! Up! Down! Up! Down!' But one standing squat is beyond them. They can barely manage to balance and now their cries are loud enough to attract teachers in further classrooms. We begin to stand in our doorways, staring.

One woman teacher comes down the steps and moves across the quad. I have never learnt her name. She has been having a difficult pregnancy. Morning sickness has dragged on and on. At assembly she sits withdrawn, avoiding conversation. Now, in full sail, she proceeds across the quad. Other women join her. She stands beside the boys and, with a movement of her hand, tells them they may lie down and let their muscles heal.

'Kelsang Gyatso,' she says, in a calm voice that carries across the quad, 'I think you may now invite the boys back into their classroom.'

Kelsang Gyatso stands to attention and faces her. They remain thus, she with a hand holding her belly, he rigid. Then he performs a military about-turn. 'Class Five boys, on your feet! To your classroom, qui-ick march.'

But marching is beyond them. They can barely manage standing. The three women support them and help them hobble into class.

Our picnic turns out to be even more tense than I had feared. Kelsang Gyatso calls for me early, we walk through the camp, over the road and up to the alewife's house. The alewife makes her living by brewing chang, the barley beer of the Himalayas. She soaks barley, sprinkles it with soda harvested from the dried-out beds of lakes in Tibet. Soda and barley are then buried in straw and after about a month the barley is disinterred and steeped in hot water. All the chang I have ever drunk has had a lemon flavour, grateful in that heat and dryness. The liquid washes away the foul-tasting scum that settles over the lips if you walk or work and the flavour cuts the stale stink from a dehydrated mouth. It also makes people relaxed and cheerful in the same way that fermented malt does.

But it does not make Kelsang Gyatso and me relaxed or cheerful. He has brought a rug, but no food. So he spreads the rug beside a backwater of the Indus and we sit on it, silently watching water stagnate.

Hindu soldiers come along and take off everything but their long, floppy underpants. They approach the water and throw in detonators. When these explode the bellies of fish appear on the surface. With curiously feminine ballet movements, the soldiers skitter through the water to gather up the fish, then dress and go.

The chang bottle is empty. We return it to the alewife. We walk towards the camp. For an hour or more we have scarcely exchanged two sentences. By the time we are passing the Jammu and Kashmir State Police barracks, I feel desperate to break the silence and say, 'I suppose tomorrow will be hot again.'

Kelsang Gyatso clenches at his picnic rug when I add that the heat can be a blessing because troublemaking children are usually the first to fall asleep. In a fever, he turns on me: 'No. They must not sleep. You must not let them.'

I have no reply. We walk on.

Then, suddenly, he says, 'Sometimes I lose my temper. I do horrible things.'

I judge that silence may be the best way of agreeing with him.

'Horrible,' he repeats. 'Horrible, horrible things.'

seven

I have never been a teacher before, and arithmetic was my worst subject at school. But now that nobody beats or mocks me for my slowness I am startled by my pleasure in the patterned beauty of the arithmetic I have to learn — startled, too, by the joy and the fretfulness the children give me, the excitement of seeing understanding spreading across faces as their brains test and accept a new idea. They also seem to be enjoying it and are soaking up the syllabus. They even grin when they attack their work.

My own dread at the thought of having to teach maths has faded. The children's successes fire me. I get delirious days when I am swept by gales of delight at the simple pleasure of handing over knowledge and seeing it arrive safely. But still I fret. I want VIA to skate through their exams and to emerge jumping with happiness at their own achievement. Crazy hope. The few children who have written themselves off will make puzzled stabs at answers and Sonam Dakpa will come out of the exam yawning at his score of ninety-five per cent. As for the middle run of kids, learning is hard work. Fifty pupils in a small room means that the crush and jostle make learning slower than it ought to be.

So I visit the headmaster. Will it be all right if I offer extra tuition to anyone who wants it? And, seeing the classrooms are locked once school ends, can the children come to my own room for extra lessons during the free time they have between sports and supper?

The headmaster stares at me. Have I said something obscene? In silence he continues to stare. He is a slight man, withdrawn inside a grey suit.

71

Never have I seen a spark in his eyes. At morning and afternoon tea when he emerges from his office to join the others, all the teachers cease their gossiping and joking. The man who is about to shove another man on the shoulder to emphasise the point of a story holds his arm still and then slowly lowers it. The murmuration among the women falls dead and they study their laps.

He keeps staring at me. Has he not understood? Must I ask again.

'Permission granted,' he says.

'Thank you, headmaster,' I say.

We are always very English with him. We never say children are studying arithmetic; they are reading mathematics. He always wears a tie. He has given up earrings. But the slits in his lobes still gape where once the weight of turquoise pulled on the gristle of his ears. Backing out, I put a shamed hand up to my throat because I have gone native. I now wear a necklace: one big speckled turquoise between two smaller lumps of coral.

Last week I saw the stones on the tray of a Tibetan hawker on the footpath behind the Leh post office.

'Da kong datso re?' I asked, which is the very respectful form of 'What do these cost?'

For a time the hawker considered my accent and she must also have wondered whether I was being mockingly deferential or just plain ignorant in using elevated words that are meant only for the ears of great grandees.

After taking her time she replied in English, 'Would it be easier for you if I answered in German or in English?' — such a delicate and perfectly aimed piece of one-upmanship that we both laughed to see her score a bull's-eye. Next day, when I wore the necklace to school, the class was enraptured. The toughest boys made me take it off so they could fondle it and envy me.

Now, with the headmaster's permission granted, I get a restrained response when I offer the children more work. But half a dozen put up their hands and, as I had feared, Tsering Lhamo is the first and keenest.

Like Sonam Dakpa, she is a solitary. She wears her hair in a bun harshly drawn back so that the skin of her brow is taut and her eyelids slitty. This tension that she applies to her face is exaggerated by the way she keeps up the old Tibetan habit of greasing her skin. Her high cheekbones glisten. The tension also limits the expressions her face can wear, but her character comes through in her body movements. She is a bustler and enthusiast.

During lessons she looks up at me, eyes crackling with the joy of being able to follow the string of foreign words that flow from my mouth. And, as she listens, her hands run on auto-pilot, busy rearranging her surroundings. With ordered precision, textbooks, pens and exercise books are laid out on her desktop. But still they require regular adjustment, a tiny shift here, a subtle smoothing, a flick to move a speck of dust.

Keeping dust on the move is urgent work for Tsering Lhamo. If I pass the camp director's rooms on my way to school I see her inside with a duster in her hand, and sometimes a shock of dismay on her face, when she discovers on his windowsill a bowl that is supposed to live on his bedside table. Her tongue tuts: will the dear man never learn? Then, puffing with the fear of arriving late, she appears in the quad laden with schoolbooks. She is so broad and squat that to get here on time she must tilt herself forward and wade angrily through the resistant air. But make it on the dot she does and straightaway hurls herself (palms pressed together, eyes heavenward) into the chant of the day.

I like to imagine her as a Western housewife, her house full of the roar of a vacuum cleaner, air thick with the smell of furniture polish, Jeyes fluid, oven cleaner and air-freshener, the carpets slick and slippery with sheets of transparent plastic floor-protectors.

If a neighbour died she would be on the doorstep before the undertaker could arrive, offering consoling gladioli from her own garden and tins of baking so that the grieving family would have something to offer sympathising visitors. Every charity in town could rely on her to stand on street corners shaking collection boxes. At annual meetings of local clubs, it would be Tsering Lhamo who cheerfully volunteered to be treasurer solely because she knew it to be the most unpopular job. And after each club's annual meeting the honorary auditor would brace himself on hearing that she had again been elected treasurer, because, for all her eagerness to learn, she seems to have a brain that is not coping with arithmetic.

She thrusts up a hand when I offer extra lessons in my room. 'Yes, sir. Me, please.'

With a different sort of grin, Dorjee Namgyal also waves an arm. Dawa Metok looks puzzled at his enthusiasm for extra arithmetic. He has no need for it. He and Dawa Metok are both doing well. But he nudges her and nods, keen, commanding. Something must click in her mind. She grins, comprehends and lifts a hand.

I stare back at them and wonder how much we understand one another. They must see the grin on my face and read it as complicity — plus an acknowledgement that I know they think I am so slack on discipline that they will be able to convert my tutorials into extra time for being together.

Not that I think I'm slack. But the violence of punishment here has made me rethink how to help kids get the best out of themselves and how to move them along the path to self-discipline. For a start, I have to admit that I am their leader. And that means I have to control myself: no outbursts, no chalk-throwing, no name-calling and no beatings.

It turns out to be an ideal that is beyond me. Soon after making up my mind not to hit kids, I lost control and strapped a boy. But it only demonstrated that thumping is pointless. Yeshi Tinley is a quick-brained little boy who keeps bursting with enthusiasm. He sits next to the girl who I think is the prettiest in the class: a vivacious face with a band of freckles across the bridge of her nose. In Yeshi Tinley I see no sign of the predatory streak that I suspect in Dorjee Namgyal. By the look of his behaviour, his mind keeps bubbling with such fresh, amusing slants on life that he can't help passing them on to the girl. She laughs. He responds with fresh jokes.

One day, though, either his brain goes into overdrive or I am on edge.

'Yeshi Tinley, you're talking too much. Calm it down.'

'Yes, sir.' He turns to her with whispered words.

'Yeshi Tinley!'

'I won't do it again, sir.'

But he does.

'Yeshi Tinley, come into the staffroom with me.'

From its nail behind the door I take down the discipline master's strap. The way I knew it as a schoolboy, teachers strap you on the hand. Yeshi Tinley has not seen it done this way. But teacher knows best, and when I tell him he puts his hand out, palm upwards. On my face I feel a tight grin — satisfaction? dismay? — as I bring the strap down with all my force.

'That hurt, sir,' he complains.

'It was bloody meant to.'

We walk back to the classroom. Within minutes he leans sideways with a new joke. I have two choices: back to the staffroom and lay into him or acknowledge that strapping had no effect and only shamed me.

So I admit its pointlessness.

My real shaming came two weeks later. The school discourages any sort of interference or even interest from parents. So it created a stir when two tatterdemalion figures pranced into the quad on the backs of little stiff-legged ponies. The visitors were real outback Tibetans, jarred by days of sitting on wooden saddles, smeared by years of going without a wash. Around their necks hung silver boxes containing holy writings. Around their waists they wore tight girdles, above which the pouches formed by the overlapping flaps of their gowns bulged with the necessities of life: snuffboxes, flintboxes, tinderboxes and wood and silver cups that would allow them to accept tea or chang from people whose tents they passed.

Hearing hoofbeats, Yeshi Tinley looked up and cried, 'My mother and father!'

Next time I went into Leh and dropped in on the Pamposh Hotel for a cup of tea, Yeshi Tinley and his parents were also there. The Pamposh Hotel sounds very grand. It is a simple teastall, maybe five paces by five, built on a street corner and open-sided to let its customers catch all movement in the bazaar.

Yeshi Tinley gave me a grin and a wave and pointed to me. His parents turned to study me. He must have explained that I was his arithmetic teacher because, when they rose to go, his father placed himself in front of me and bowed saying, 'Geler-la', which means 'honoured teacher'.

I felt shrivelled — so much respect after the way I had treated his son. Worse came. When I went to pay, the boy behind the counter waved me away. 'That old scarecrow paid for you.'

eight

Life grows curiouser and curiouser. Here among prayer wheels, temples and chants I find I have turned into a regular churchgoer, for two reasons. The first is a lost dictionary-maker. The second reason dates back to 1863.

This is the year when the Moravian Church, which is a cousin of the Lutherans, decides to send three bachelor missionaries to Tibet. Already the Pope has sent Portuguese missionaries there, but Moravians have no time for the Pope — he had their founder burnt at the stake — so they decide to cleanse Tibetan minds of all lingering traces of popery.

The Moravian Church has been in the missionary business since 1732, so its bosses are not green: they know what the three bachelors will face. Tibet will be tough. Geography, bandits and an official suspicion of visitors will make sure of that. But the greater the difficulties the Moravians face, the more brightly will they burnish Christ's lustre. And their own.

The three bachelors' biggest difficulty comes during their first winter. They are snow-stuck in a gorge somewhere to the south of Ladakh, a gorge so narrow, according to a Ladakhi whom I meet at the little Moravian church at Leh, that you can kick a football from one side to the other, meaning that only briefly at midday can the missionaries see the sun flit between the mountains. Here the Moravians shelter in a farmhouse until the spring of 1864, when they start moving north again. Their instructions are to turn right once they hit the Indus. Instead they turn left. They are only a day's walk from Leh, and when they get there they stop.

Perhaps they decide that the king's palace, vast upon its crag, matches reports of the Dalai Lama's stupendous palace at Lhasa. Or perhaps they just feel they have walked far enough. In any case they set up their mission station. They sow cabbage, kholrabi and radish seeds, they erect an observatory, build a church, start a school, catalogue important buildings and write home to say that they would be obliged if someone could send three agreeable young Christian spinsters.

Three sturdy girls take ship, round the Cape of Good Hope, land in India, travel north and strike out to walk across the Himalayas. They make it to Leh, find the three bachelors and, as people used to say, settle down to making the best of things. Their husbands' surnames are Redslob, Francke and — remember this one — Heidi.

For the three brides and the three husbands, missionary work turns into a life sentence. They never leave Ladakh. Today their bodies lie lined up in the walled-in Christian cemetery in an out-of-the-way gully on the upriver fringe of Leh.

Ladakh's rocks are stony ground for Christianity and their mission is no great success. The people listen politely enough to the Moravians but prefer to remain Buddhists and take the chance of a good reincarnation rather than convert to Christianity and face the near-certainty of eternal hellfire.

Neither, though, is the Moravian mission a complete failure. Today the observatory has become a wreck, but the church still stands. Mid-morning every Sunday its tinny bell tinkles among poplars and apricot trees and inside the building a Dutch-speaking Tibetan, Pastor Hershey, sings God's praises, accompanying himself on his guitar. Hershey is also headmaster of the Moravian school and is a member of a committee that is translating the Bible into Tibetan.

'Even all the begats?' I asked when first we met.

'Of course', he replied and reeled off a sample of the words he was working on: 'And when Baal-hanan died Hadad reigned in his stead and the name of his city was Pai, and his wife's name was Mehetabel . . .'

Over time I learned to envy Hershey's special standing at the State Bank of India. Since my first visit to Ladakh I have seen the Leh branch of the State Bank grow. The first time I went there to cash a traveller's cheque, the bank was a couple of desks underneath the staircase of a back-street building. Even at noon, the staff needed a kerosene lamp hanging from the underside of the stairs to see by. Today the bank is a proud single-storeyed mud-brick building facing the main bazaar. At its front door stands a corporal armed with a rifle that is chained to his belt so that he cannot be disarmed by robbers, and to emphasise the attention the bank gives to keeping money safe, its front wall bears a bold notice: 'No Entry with Firearms'.

So they have security sewn up, but not efficiency. On days when the bank is running at top speed we customers must stand around for thirty-five minutes while our traveller's cheques are given the treatment. I hand over my passport and a traveller's cheque and in return I am given a numbered brass plaque that overlaps my palm. The bank teller places my cheque and passport on a desk. There a clerk writes the details in a ledgerbook and places the cheque and my passport in his out tray. The clerk is too lofty to carry my bits of paper to the next desk. That is the peon's job. But the peon is usually making tea, filling inkwells or running errands in the bazaar.

Eventually, though, the peon moves the bits of paper to the desk of a second clerk, who now enters the same details in a daybook. When the peon empties the second clerk's out tray, the papers are carried to a third desk where yet another clerk works out the rate of exchange and enters the details into a leather-bound journal and fills in a form — name, date, passport number — saying how much I am to be given in rupees.

Now everything is ready for the final stage. The clerk files carbon copies of the form and puts the top copy, my traveller's cheque and passport into a tray for the peon to collect. The peon walks to a thief-proof cage constructed of wire netting and pushes the bits of paper through a slot. The cage is lighted by a kerosene pressure-lamp and by its glow the cashier peers at the serial number that has been given to my transaction and shouts the number at the top of his voice. I look at my brass plaque and glow: my number has come up. Now I can go to the cashier and exchange my plaque for money and passport.

I notice, though, that Pastor Hershey gets instant treatment. Instead of standing waiting on the customers' side of the counter, he ducks underneath it, sits beside the clerk and does his business in five minutes. As well as the bank, Pastor Hershey has the army in his hands. The general of the Northern Army is a Christian and Hershey occasionally scrounges a ride on an army jeep so that he can carry the word to out-of-the-way villages.

So I think of Hershey when I start receiving letters and telegrams urging me to busy myself and discover a lost lexicographer.

She had been working in England on a dictionary and when that job finished she accepted work on another dictionary being produced in Australia. A sober and orderly person, and dutiful in writing to her mother, she was last heard of in Srinagar where she was trying to organise a trip to Ladakh before heading off for Sydney. After a long silence from her, the lexicographer's mother, who comes from my home town, wrote begging me to find her.

A big order; there's a lot of countryside out there. And not a welcome order because I am feeling devoted to the children and have become obsessed with the idea that I can get them all to swoop through their exams with ease and grace. I shall not abandon them to go looking for someone who may never have got up here. Then again, I must do something. So the first job is to discover whether the lost lexicographer ever did get to Ladakh. I think of Pastor Hershey and his friendship with the Christian general.

One of the army's jobs is to run a roadside checkpoint near Kargil. On a scrap of flat land that looks as if it was chosen for its absolute desolation stands an army tent containing a trestle table at which soldiers sit. Between the road and the entrance to the tent a pathway has been made and in proper army style the pathway has been edged with whitewashed boulders.

Buses making the two-day journey from Srinagar to Leh are forced to stop here. The driver then offers his passengers a choice. They are supposed to line up outside the tent and go in to give names and passport numbers to the seated soldiers. If, however, they want to buck the regulations, they may stay in the bus, but will have to sit on the floor where the soldiers will not notice them. If the lost lexicographer got out of the bus and gave her name to the soldiers at the trestle table, their list of passengers will carry a record of her arrival in Ladakh and perhaps her departure.

But how to get that information for her mother?

I call on Pastor Hershey and ask if he can use his friendship with the general to get soldiers to go through their checkpoint lists and see whether the lexicographer has come and gone. He agrees. And next time I am in town he says the general has ordered a search of the lists. So all I now have to do is to hike down the valley every Sunday, because that is my day off, join Hershey's church service and afterwards ask if he has any news from the general.

In theory, I could have used the refugee camp phone to keep in touch with the pastor. But this is India and the telephone can be the slowest way of getting a message across. The system collapses so often that, even in Delhi, big companies hire messengers to run around the city with notes rather than risk the delays and frustrations of trying to ring through.

For weeks the camp telephone line to Leh has been on the blink and Jigme Kunga has been in a fury over its failure. In the end he went down to Leh to complain to the postmaster that, even though he had bribed the telephone linemen, weeks had passed and they had done nothing to earn their bribes by fixing the fault. According to Jigme Kunga, the postmaster was outraged and wondered what the world was coming to. Had people forgotten the meaning of honesty? He was ashamed that any of his men would take a bribe and not do the work. He promised to stir them up and to insist that, in future, when they accept a bribe, they must do the work promptly.

Jigme Kunga is convinced that my weekly hikes to church are a waste of time. The lost lexicographer, he tells me, is sure to be dead. By now, an army patrol will have raped her and thrown her body over a cliff. He may be right. But still I keep my weekly date with Pastor Hershey to see if the army has any record of her.

I also go to the post office and join the ruck of people trying to buy stamps. When I catch the eye of the man behind the counter I shout out the lost lexicographer's surname. He reaches into a pigeon-hole, extracts letters for her and hands them to me. I take them away and wonder whether I am a thief. Or am I just collecting evidence of her possible movements? The fact that she had not collected her mail suggests she never made it up here, or so I tell her mother when I post the letters back to her.

One Sunday on my way to church I climb a high wall at the upriver end of Leh and jump down into the cemetery — the Christian cemetery.

Ladakhi Buddhists don't have cemeteries. Away from their houses, they build little mud chimneys on the ground, about the size of a sixty-litre drum. Then they truss their dead in a sitting position, jam them into the mud chimney, get a fire going underneath and start basting the body with yak butter, which is necessary if they are to keep the corpse burning because Ladakhis are as skinny as hares and have no fat of their own to feed a flame. The buttered flesh burns away. A few big bones remain. When everything has cooled, the living clean out the homemade crematorium and chuck the bones away, leaving the chimney looking neat for the next death.

Ladakhi Muslims, who are beginning to outnumber Buddhists, bury their dead in their own cemetery. The grave markers, each made to the same pattern, spread on and on across the desert until they lap the Christian cemetery's stone walls, inside which lies a clashing jumble of headstones, each one different as if competing to catch God's attention — which is surprising, because the Christian God must look upon Ladakhi believers as his special pets. There are only eighty-one of them. And their cemetery shows how delicately Christianity is poised between survival and extinction: such a tiny harvest of headstones to show for more than a century of missionary work.

Not that the first Moravians limited themselves to preaching and teaching. In 1880 the Franckes, the Redslobs and the Heidis were joined by a young doctor with a famous name. He opened the Moravian medical dispensary and one of his regular spring tasks was to nip off the frostbitten fingers and toes of traders from Chinese Turkestan who, eager to lead the first caravan of the year over the Karakoram Range, started out too soon and became trapped in late snowstorms.

The doctor lasted only eleven years in Leh. In 1891 he died there of a fever. And it is because of his death that I have climbed the wall of the locked cemetery and have dropped down into the graveyard itself, thinking that it may make a curious detour as I walk to church to enquire about the lost lexicographer. The effort turns out to be worthwhile. I find the young doctor's headstone and read his name: Karl Marx.

My cemetery crawl makes me late for church but still early enough to witness a miracle: a Muslim man is converting to Christianity. He is switching because of one of the two Texan women who are visiting Leh.

They are sisters called Leeann and Linda. Both are keen jump-for-Jesus types and they have been wandering around town with big bags of sweets which they hand out to children to demonstrate how God loves everybody. One day they even came out to the refugee camp and, uninvited, entered classrooms to distribute sweets. When they came into my room I asked if they would mind waiting outside until playtime. One of them replied 'Oh, my!' in a way that made me feel pompous and unbending.

A few days later, when I met the two Texans in town, I was still feeling in two minds: of course I was right to kick them out and of course I might also have been right if I had let them take five minutes of class time. So when we met in town I tried to make up by letting them tell me all about themselves.

Three weeks beforehand, they said, they had never heard of Leh, let alone Ladakh. They weren't even all that positive where India was. But Linda had just come out of a treatment centre that handled people's drinking problems and was in counselling when — Whammee! — she heard God's voice saying they must both come right on up here to Leh. And, said Leeann, it just goes to show how right God is. Because. There. Is. Absolutely. No. Drink. Available. Here.

I nod soberly.

But because autumn is coming on, I ask whether God dropped any useful hints about bringing clothes suitable for minus-forty-degree winters. For a second they look shaken, then tell me, buoyantly, that God will provide. He always does. Or maybe he will send them somewhere warmer where it is equally impossible to find booze.

In Leh, Linda and Leeann look like escapers from a freak show. Across their faces both wear broad slashes of scarlet lipstick. In a community that goes in for little washing and much manual work, their hands are soft, unstained and lotioned. Their hair still looks prinked and permed. They smell of the beauty salon. Gold rings cover their fingers. Among people who are gentle and reserved, they shout and wave across the street. They call to strange children and advance upon them yelling, 'Bonbons, bonbons!'

Last Sunday they arrived in church with a strange man, brown-skinned but with a clearly European face. Linda and he were holding hands. He wore an oatmeal-coloured sports coat and a tangerine scarf. In the Leh church the sexes always sit apart, men cross-legged on one side, women cross-legged on the other. Last Sunday the sisters and the man sat together on the men's side and seemed not to notice the way Ladakhis tensed and shrank into themselves on seeing their own customs broken. This Sunday the three of them sit together on the women's side. Although I arrive late I notice they are still getting affronted glances. But not from Pastor Hershey.

Today, he announces in English, Josuf will become a Christian. He makes a sign inviting the man in the tangerine scarf to come forward.

And so he does. But when he reaches the altar steps he tells the pastor in a clear, level voice, which we can all hear, that his own English is not good enough to understand perfectly all that may be said. Turkish is his best language. But he has worked in Germany. So his German is better than his English. Is there any chance, he asks, that a German speaker is present who could translate the pastor's English?

We all look around doubtfully. A German? *Here?* But we need not have doubted. A tall, well-fleshed man in his fifties is rising to his feet. He wears a well-cut suit, an expensive shirt and tie. Everything about him suggests one of the less flashy professions. A surgeon? A successful but honest accountant?

'Heidi,' he announces. 'My name is Heidi.'

If he had been white-bearded, long-haired and gowned and had announced that he was God, he could scarcely have been given a better reception. Bodies lift with a jolt. Every head swings. Delight and adoration settle upon faces.

Heidi acknowledges the effect of his announcement. 'Yes, I am a grandson. I visit.'

Now he swings into German. Josuf replies. Heidi speaks again. Josuf responds. Heidi announces, 'Pastor, he speaks well German. I translate.'

In English, the Dutch-speaking Tibetan invites the Turk to acknowledge Christ as his redeemer. The missionary's grandson turns the question into German, and in German the Turk responds. Heidi gives his answers in English. The catechism of the Turk rolls on and, when it is done, Hershey makes the mark of the cross on Josuf's brow. Then Josuf turns, beams at Linda and, with little skippy movements, hurries back to her side. She hugs him. Pastor Hershey bows at Herr Heidi. Herr Heidi bows and sits.

Now Hershey drops back into the routine of his normal Sunday service. But he need not have bothered. The congregation has been touched by a miracle — another Heidi here unannounced to save a soul — and upon this Sunday the people want to bask in the miracle: they need no more talk from Pastor Hershey.

nine

Last week a letter arrived from a friend: 'What on earth possessed you to hide like this away from all the action? You are missing so much.'

One of the things I had missed, she said, was a birthday party at which a wife had started shouting at her husband, accusing him of chasing after little boys when everyone knew he was spending all his time and energy on his wife's best friend. And after the party someone else I knew crashed his car and had a leg amputated.

Okay, my life here can't compete, but I have not been the total hermit. On Saturday I went out to dinner at the palace. Yvonne and Mathilde, the palace cleaning ladies, asked me, and their invitation included the strict command: Bring your own bowl and spoon.

Yvonne is from Switzerland and Mathilde, who is rounder and jollier and smokes a pipe, is from Germany. They have installed themselves in an abandoned palace at Shey about five kilometres up the valley because the palace is so handy to their work. Yvonne and Mathilde are art restorers sent here by some Swiss archaeological society that is trying to preserve Ladakh's treasures. Next door to the palace is a half-abandoned temple that is constructed around a fairly ordinary two-storey statue of the Buddha figure called Sakyamuni. The heads of the royal dynasty have had the responsibility of keeping butter-lamps burning for several hundred years at the feet of the statue — so many centuries of flame and oily smuts that when you climb to a mezzanine floor which lies at the same height as the shoulders of the statue you find the walls thick with soot. It seems at first to be of a uniform blackness. But stand hard up against the wall, look along it at an acute angle against the light, and faintly a raised pattern becomes visible.

Yvonne and Mathilde have set up a tiny Japanese electricity generator on a flat roof of the temple and all day its petrol engine rattles the air so that inside floodlights can wash the black walls with brilliance. All day Yvonne and Mathilde dab at the walls with cotton wool soaked in weak acetate. Then gently, gently, they rub the work with soft breadcrumbs from loaves that a Muslim baker prepares especially for them. In one summer they have cleaned perhaps a tenth of the entire wall surface and, instead of having to stare at oily blackness, they can now run their eyes over a fraction of a mural that is emerging with charm and brilliance.

Most ancient Ladakhi paintings I have seen are a delight because of

Yvonne and Mathilde's palace on the right, the temple where they work on the left.

their naïvety and the dotty devotion to detail that fired the dead painters. The most outstanding wall paintings are like wallpaper: tiny repeat patterns in which each motif is reduced to the size of a postage stamp. Look closely, though, and the pattern of these ancient paintings is not truly repetitive.

Each tiny picture is different. The Buddha appears in his many forms, sages sit advising kings, princesses arrive bearing food, princes lead troops to war, the dreadful blue bull of the Tibetan hell punishes dead men by buggering them until they scream. And each tiny painting looks as if it were done with a two-hair brush.

But here in the Shey temple, the work emerging from the soot is large and loose and free, and the artist, instead of working nose to wall in stiff stipples has stood back, held his arm away from his body and swung his hand in easy sweeps. And, when first he stepped into the temple and looked at the blank wall, he knew how to organise and fill a space and how to turn a flat surface into life.

Yvonne and Mathilde have uncovered a big, bold Buddha riding a raging tiger, the Buddha's face serene even though the tiger twists and turns as it tries to bite off the Buddha's foot. Nearby a second Buddha wears a gown of glowing brilliancy worked in gold-leaf filigree of lacy delicacy. The whole figure has the same easy grace of posture as in Botticelli's *The Birth of Venus* but, rather than having a shell to ride on, the Buddha sprouts a foam of peony blossom around and below the hem of his gown. A peony in the deserts of Ladakh? Not in nature, I think. This mural can only be the work of a travelling artist bringing memories of lusher gardens in richer, moister soils.

Work on the mural has nudged Yvonne and Mathilde into top-level diplomacy. The queen of Ladakh owns both the ruined palace and the half-abandoned temple and it is her lifetime duty to keep on paying for the butter burning in the lamps at Sakyamuni's feet — the same butter-lamps that continue to send soot skyward until it clings again to the mural that Yvonne and Mathilde are cleaning.

When the queen visited Yvonne and Mathilde to see the work they are doing, they explained the obvious: the holy soot from downstairs is again beginning to ruin the work of piety they have uncovered on the upper walls. They think they saw on the queen's face the recognition that she can't have it both ways. Either the lamps go or the mural will once again disappear. From the rundown look of the palace at Stok where the queen lives, the remnants of the royal family have no money to spare and they might be able to live better if they could get out of their duty to provide butter for the lamps. Protection of these gorgeous paintings might offer an excuse to end the temple's butter ration. But rank has its duties. And if the queen ducks one royal obligation, does it follow that some of the sheen falls from her nobility? Or is discussion about the butter-lamps impossible because religion imposes an absolute duty to burn butter — a duty that no reasoning can remove?

My own guess is that the mural is eighteenth-century Chinese and that it took less than 200 years to obliterate it. At that rate, there is no rush to decide to lose face by abolishing the butter-lamps and, anyway, help may be on its way.

Further up the valley towards Hemis Monastery a dam is slowly being built and, when electricity is flowing from it, the Swiss archaeological rescuers may present the queen with boxes of those flickering light bulbs that people use in bogus ye olde pubs, and the Swiss may be able to persuade the pious and cash-strapped royals that white-hot filaments give off the same degree of sanctity as does burning butter.

But until then, here it is, Saturday night, and I am at Shey clambering up the track that leads to the ridge of the crag on which the palace ruins stand. Eventually I reach the palace gates, my bowl and my spoon in my hands, and I am staring at the ghastly void that lies between the gateway and the palace door. Once a broad path from the gate to the door used to cross the flat roof of an underground chamber. But the roof has fallen in and, with it, all the pathway.

The only vestige of the path is a ledge of dressed stone jutting from a wall. Pressing my back against the wall, I fumble my feet along the ledge and presently I hold out a trembling hand which shakes so much that it takes almost no extra effort to knock on the door of Shey palace. The door opens inwards and there stand Yvonne and Mathilde, who have grown so accustomed to using the ledge, running along it several times a day, that they smile at the terror on my face.

They have prepared a dazzling dinner — dazzling because they have left their electricity generator running, they have hauled their spotlights over from the temple and down into the main reception room of the palace and there they have created a dining table by mounting planks on legs made out of sun-dried bricks, and over the planks they have spread glittering white linen — well, not really linen, just a bedsheet. Not since coming to Ladakh have I seen such light — and what a grand room it is to fill with light! On the walls traces of painted scenes still cling, on the rafters painted geometric patterns stand out.

Yvonne and Mathilde, who live perfectly well on local food, possess worried friends who keep posting them tinned delicacies, which they have saved up for our feast: hams, pâtés, cheeses, conserves, pickled vegetables. And I, why, I am contributing to this evening of luxurious indulgence by bringing a bottle of Indian wine.

The name on the label is Purple Princess Vermouth, which ought to have been a warning. When we pour some, the smell suggests methylated spirits that has been doctored with herbal flavourings to justify the claim on the label. After one sip our glasses remain untouched and when the full moon is well risen and offering enough light for my walk back down the valley, Yvonne and Mathilde beg me to take the Purple Princess away from their palace.

Next day I write letters, mark children's exercises, walk, eat lunch and have a nap, from which I am woken by a knock on the door, which advertises that the visitors cannot be Tibetans. And neither they are. They are a bunch of medical students from Dublin. They are greatly agitated. Walking across boggy grazing between Shey and Choglamsar, they saw a dead baby in a stream. Its ankles were wired to a stone.

They remembered that on their way upstream, they had passed the Indo-Tibetan Border Police camp. So they turned back and reported to the sentry that they had stumbled on a murder. The sentry responded by putting out his right hand, palm downward, and rocking the hand from side to side, meaning: Go away, you're not allowed in an army camp.

The Dubliners grew angry and refused to go away. The sentry rang the adjutant's office. The subaltern on duty appeared. Murder! Drowned baby! You've got to do something! The subaltern managed not to grow excited. He said the best thing to do would be to turn around again and to go back upstream. After two or three kilometres they would find the Jammu and Kashmir Police barracks. Murdered babies were their business.

But the Jammu and Kashmir Police said: This is only our barracks. This is where we rest. The station is downstream in Leh. Turn round again. Walk down to Leh. There'll be someone on duty there.

Somehow the Dubliners had heard that there was a pink-skinned foreigner living in the Tibetan refugee camp over the road from the barracks, and they thought he might know what they ought to do to make the police interested in murder. So they knock on my door. Their faces lighten. At last, someone who will understand.

But I grow resentful. I am still swamped by love for Ladakhis. On my previous walking trips I have seen them gentle and jolly with their children. I have felt their hospitality. I have seen how hard they slog to stay alive. I do not want to believe any of them would drown a baby. I just don't want to know. But I understand the Dubliners' bafflement at running into policemen who don't get excited over murder. So I make tea and rearrange my face to look indignant and sympathetic.

The tea calms the Dubliners a bit. I tell them the best thing is to walk down to Leh and go to the police station.

One asks, 'And where might the police station be, man?'

'I don't know,' I say, and restrain myself from adding, 'You could always ask a policeman.'

'And are you saying we must walk all that way to report a murder?'

Their appetite is for noise and instant action, for cellphones and radio alerts, sirens, patrol cars crashing through red lights at intersections, tyres squealing on corners, loudhailers ordering crowds to stand back, brakes, car doors flying open, armed policemen running with pistols. Reluctantly, they set off in a babble of disputation.

I do not shut the door on them because here comes Dorjee Gyaltsen. He, too, has seen a dead body. He and Dolkar and the children were walking up the valley to visit his parents when they saw a run-over dog lying beside the road. Dolkar began worrying about what sort of reincarnation it would have. What if it turned into a worm or a rat? She grew so upset that she could not carry on, so they turned back and went home. There Dolkar became so distraught that Dorjee Gyaltsen took seven grains of barley into the palm of one hand. (Here, to make sure I get the point, he lifts both hands, with seven fingers pointing at me.) One by one Dolkar placed the seven grains in his ear and he recited incantations designed to bring the dead dog an improved future.

'Maybe it will be born a man,' I say.

'Well, a woman at least.' He gives a giggle as if he knows he is being naughty and that modern men no longer make this sort of joke.

I pour two rums. 'Here's to a better reincarnation.'

After three rums Dorjee Gyaltsen begins to believe that his incantations and the barley in his ear are beginning to do their stuff and he floats home to Dolkar.

While my potatoes boil for dinner, I reread the letter — 'You are missing so much.'

ten

I have had my VA science class taken away from me. And I don't think I'm doing too well either with my English lessons for class VII.

When I arrived and was given VA for science, the school science master had got the children up to the point where they were working their way towards the second law of thermodynamics: 'It is impossible for an unaided self-acting machine to convey heat from one body to another at a higher temperature.' I thought it would be sufficient to simplify the law and teach that heat moves from the hotter to the colder body and then to go on to look at how easily heat moves through, say, iron and how reluctantly it moves through mud.

In my innocence, this looked an easy job. I worked out how I could make the class feel with their own hands heat moving into a colder body. I could set up a demonstration so that they could watch heat moving. Then I could show them how to feel for themselves the speed of heat moving through concrete and how slowly it would pass through soil.

But quickly I felt like brave Galileo standing before the Inquisition, baffled at how confidently faith can override fact, because the science I was teaching was in collision with the children's religion — not, I think, with Buddhism but with the animism that preceded Buddhism. Before Buddhism, Tibetans knew that spirits inhabited and governed inanimate materials. Today, I suspect, animism survives: it has invaded Buddhism and lives within its shelter.

For example, Ladakhis still perform springtime archery contests designed to charm and appease the spirit of the soil so that he will refrain from punishing ploughmen who attack the ground that is his home. Likewise, mountain passes are ruled by spirits which demand tribute from all who use them. On ridges stand cairns of stones and all travellers must bribe the spirit to let them pass. People pay their dues by adding a fresh stone or starting a new cairn in honour of the spirit of the pass. And spirits rule rivers. From bridges flutter strips of cloth printed with prayers to encourage river spirits to do no harm to people who have sought their protection.

Faith in spirits is nothing for us to laugh at. Watch a battalion of atheist astrophysicists walking along a footpath and see how many avoid walking under ladders to save themselves from the anger of the ladder spirit. But faith in spirits — I was to learn — can completely baffle the efforts of science teachers.

VA's classroom had a concrete floor and mud-brick walls, an ideal laboratory for demonstrating thermodynamics. So I explained how everything that the children could see was, as near as damn, at the same temperature. The floor was just as cold as their desks. Their chair legs were as cold as the mud walls. The walls were as cold as the floor. And everything was about the same temperature as the air because as soon as any one thing grew warmer, its extra heat would flow into the other things.

The only material in the room that constantly remained warmer than anything else was our own flesh and we could easily use its heat to feel how warmth flows from the hotter body to a colder body. I got them to crouch around the classroom walls with one hand on a mud wall and the other hand on the concrete floor.

Could they feel their hands growing colder?

They all nodded.

Okay, why were their hands feeling colder? Could it be because the heat in their hands was flowing into the colder walls and floor?

Please, sir, it is because the spirits are sucking the heat out.

No. No. No — and I told them again that heat moves from the warmer to the colder. Have they not felt it themselves sitting by a fire? It's not because they are sucking the heat out. If they grab a burning stick, the heat will keep coming into their hand whether they want it to or not. Wanting heat has nothing to do with it. Understand?

Heads nod.

Okay, which hand feels colder? The hand on the concrete floor? Or the hand on the mud-brick wall?

Please, sir, the hand on the floor.

Right. You've got it. Now, why does the hand on the concrete floor feel colder? Could it be that the heat in your hand moves more quickly into concrete than into mud? Would that make the hand on the concrete lose more heat than the hand on the mud? Has anyone got an answer?

Please, sir, it is because the spirit in the concrete is greedier.

That night, after a hefty rum, my own spirits began slowly to rise after my failure and I began to work out a demonstration that could not fail to show how heat moves.

Next morning, at the carpenter's shop, I scrounged a short length of steel reinforcing rod and five nails and promised to return them all after school. With blobs of molten wax from a burning candle, I stuck the nails along the length of the steel rod and, in front of the children, held one end of the rod in the candle flame.

Now watch, I say: The heat from the candle flame is moving into the steel rod, it is going to melt the first blob of wax and the nail will fall off. On cue the wax melts. The nail falls. And I try not to look too self-satisfied.

Keep watching, I say. The heat is still moving along the rod, soon it will melt the next bit of wax and the next nail will fall.

With a fine metallic ping the nail falls on to the concrete floor.

Oh, clever me! The children are enthralled. They are gobbling information out of my hand. They are so enchanted that not a breath can be heard and every eye is on the reinforcing rod. What a brilliant teacher I must be.

The third nail falls, the fourth, the fifth. I put down the rod and blow out the candle.

Okay, kids, let's talk about what we've seen. Why do you think all the nails fell off in order? First it was the nail nearest the candle, then the second nail, then the third and so on. Does anyone think it might have been because the heat was moving along the rod and melting the wax blobs one by one?

Please, sir, it was the spirit in the iron that made the nails fall.

I am undaunted. Day by day I dream up gripping, creative ways of showing them what they are supposed to be learning. And, day by day, they tell me that everything I show them is the work of spirits.

Eventually, the headmaster gives the class back to the school science master. I am humiliated. Passing the VA classroom, I stand below an open window and spy on how he teaches. He sits by his desk. On his knees lies the open textbook and he reads to the children: 'It is impossible for an unaided self-acting machine to convey heat . . .'

They recite back: 'It is impossible . . .'

'Right. That boy there, you stand up and say the words.'

A chair scrapes and a solitary treble repeats the second law of thermodynamics.

'Good. Remember the words and you will pass your examination.'

The English students of class VII have different difficulties. Most of their time at school they have been taught in Hindi. Now English is the language of instruction. They are at ease in Hindi but English remains a foreign language; they can manage, but only slowly and with care. And with diffidence. They still hate to risk it out loud.

If only I had a tape-recorder. The magic of having their own voices played back would have them jostling to be the next to speak into the machine. The shyness barrier would collapse. But, even with a tape-recorder, their English lessons would be uphill all the way if only because the textbook does not match their own lives. The book was produced by the remote and lofty savants of the Indian Educational Institute, who seem more keen to show off their learning than to help the students.

Not that it can be easy to produce a textbook for all India. Down south at Cape Comorin, India is like Samoa with elephants; up here it is like Tibet with warplanes. In between lies everything else: deserts, cities, dank and chilly highlands, plains melting in killer heat. The people of India lack one common thread of experience that tells them they live in India. Inevitably, our textbook is crammed with references that have no meaning up here in the mountains.

We start off with an extract from a biography of Gandhi. Here he is, a young lawyer in South Africa acting as assistant to a barrister who is suing for the payment of a debt. The court case has already begun and Gandhi is idly running his eyes down the statement of claim. Suddenly something clicks: someone has made a mistake in adding up the money that the defendant is supposed to owe the man who has hired Gandhi and the senior barrister to recover.

It is not a big mistake but — and here is the point of the story — Gandhi says the claim must be amended, otherwise they are asking for money to which their customer has no right.

The barrister is outraged. He cannot believe that Gandhi could suggest they should admit a mistake. He tells Gandhi that his idea is pure folly. The debtor's lawyer would sense a weakness in their case. Admit one mistake, and the judge and jury would suspect more errors.

But Gandhi insists. They cannot demand more money than their customer is owed. That would not be honest.

What has honesty got to do with it? We're not here for honesty, says the barrister. We're here to win the case.

Again Gandhi insists. He cannot work on a false claim. He will have to walk off the case.

The barrister blows up. Walk off? It's not you who's going to walk off, sonny boy. I am going to walk off. I'm not going to work with a loony

Class VII, the school seniors — 'Please, sir, what is
an island?'

like you. You do it your own way. You'll lose a perfectly straightforward
case. You're building up quite a good reputation, Mr Gandhi, but now
you're trying to ruin it for the sake of a shilling or two. But you do it your
way. And don't say I didn't warn you.

The barrister departs. Gandhi amazes the court by reducing the
statement of claim. And he wins the case.

Class VII and I struggle over the text for more than a week. They are
bright, questioning and charming young men and women. As the children
of herding families living on the western tip of the great Western Plain of
Tibet, they must have survival skills I cannot even imagine. They speak
more languages than I know; they write in three alphabets.

In their parents' yak-hair tents they had no need to know about courts, lawyers or unpaid bills. In trying to work our way through the Gandhi text, they and I face one another across a gulf of incomprehension and nothing I can do brings our minds closer; nothing I can explain puts the light of understanding in their eyes.

Finally the head boy of the school stands up. 'Please, sir, we are not understanding. Let us try the next lesson.'

I nod. We all turn the page in our textbooks. I feel as relieved as they seem.

But not for long. The next lesson is an extract from *The Tempest* and instantly we are lost again. Act One, Scene I: Prospero, Duke of Milan, is shipwrecked on an island after a storm at sea.

Please, sir, what is a sea?

Please, sir, what is a Milan?

Please, sir, what is an island?

eleven

'I wish you were my father', says Astrid, who is an anthropologist from Australia. Her father is Norwegian, as is her mother. The mother lives in Western Australia, divorced from Astrid's raging, flailing father, who has gone to live in Sydney with all the red and crinkled emptiness of Australia holding him apart from his family.

I suppose Astrid means well, but I do not want to be her father. Occasionally I want to be her seducer.

I can see precisely how I would have my way with her. Down from the mountains above the queen's palace I would gallop on the back of a long-paced dappled grey. From my shoulders would stream a cloak of some luxurious but serviceable material. A merino-cashmere blend might do.

Astrid and Tenzing, the Tibetan lover she wants to take back to Australia with her, would be strolling along the road through Choglamsar when first they heard my horse's restless hooves drumming on the bridge over the Indus. Excited by the beat, they would stand unmoving, unable to take their eyes from the dash and swirl of my approach. Astrid's heart would thrill as she saw my black and hawklike eyes upon her. (Actually hawks' eyes are a topaz yellow but maybe she doesn't know that.) In one easy movement I would bend from the saddle, curl a muscled arm around her waist and lift her from the ground.

At this point, the seduction of Astrid goes fuzzy. There I am with one melting and eager anthropologist held in one arm and nowhere to put her. The easy answer is to dump her on the horse's neck. But horses hate that. They lower their heads until the unwelcome passenger slides off. Astrid really needs to be behind me, with urgent hands either clasped around my waist or busy with lewd stroking. But I cannot see how even the most lithe and powerful horseman can swing any lady anthropologist around behind himself and settle her on the horse's rump without finishing up with the lady facing back to front.

No matter. The moment of seduction is perfectly clear in my imagination. On a balcony of my castle built high on a crag overlooking the queen's frumpy palace, Astrid and I sprawl on silken cushions watching my pet lammergeiers — also known as bearded vultures — circling in the sky while we toy with beakers of chilled riesling. Slowly she eases her body out of her clothes and moans: 'Take me. Take me now.'

When I am not refining the details of Astrid's seduction, and when I am not resenting her tactlessness for thinking of me as a father rather than as some unattainably perfect lover, I am smarting from the kill-cock disdain she shows towards my suggestions about her work.

She is living over the road in Choglamsar with Tenzing and doing postgraduate study on whether the lamas screw the peasants. Everybody believes the monasteries possess huge granaries filled with barley and that in the villages outside their walls they also own great barley fields which poor people must cultivate for the monks. So the lamas have got it all worked out: they will not work and they shall not starve.

When a bad winter comes, though, the poor villagers — or so people say — must beg for food. But the abbots refuse help unless the peasants pledge future crops: 'You wanna kilo now? You gimme two kilos in the autumn.' One result is that the monasteries have developed a reputation as evil usurers who, beneath surface appearances of piety and poverty, are the real owners of Ladakh, extorting food from the lowly and obedience from all by their threats of disagreeable reincarnations. Astrid's job is to find out if the people really are forced to give food they cannot spare to lamas who have more than they can eat.

Here in India debts that run from generation to generation and impose slavery on the poorest people are a national curse. Another is well-meaning ineffectualness: child labour has been made unlawful. Still it continues. And government decrees have abolished both the dowry system and the Untouchable caste. But Untouchable babies are still born to be outcasts and new brides, squatting as they cook on kerosene pressure-stoves, still have petrol chucked over their stoves and their saris so that their husbands' families can keep the dowries when the women burn to death. And still debtors' children are given as slaves. They work to pay the interest on their parents' debt.

Astrid and I are discussing her work and what line of inquiry she can take. I suggest she gets the text of a law that I think is called the Cancellation of Debt Act. I suspect its purpose is to end generation-unto-generation debts and thereby end child slavery. I also suspect it is one of those laws that members of parliament like to pass, partly to make themselves feel good and partly because they have grown so big-headed and so isolated from reality that they seriously believe that if they write a law against evil all naughtiness will pass away.

I argue that if the law says what I think it does and if Astrid finds that abbots break it by screwing families for interest in perpetuity, then she will be able to write a stronger finding than if she has no starting point other than her own opinion that slavery through perpetual debt is evil.

When I say this she rages. How dare I argue for slavery? I am a brutal idiot. And what difference does a law make? No one needs to track down some silly law. I am as bad as her academic supervisor, worse. He is always telling her to consult original documents. But if she can learn from families trapped in eternal poverty how much grain they have to give the local monastery, then she has all the facts she needs — and better facts than she can get by copying from bits of paper. As for me, I have the soul of a sanitary inspector. No vision. No warmth. No intellect. Only a crazed love for looking up books and filling in forms. I am the same as the Nazi office-workers at Buchenwald who listed each day's tally of gassed Jews and made inventories of gold tooth-fillings.

At this she gives a final glare and dashes from my room, trying to slam the door as she goes. But no slam comes. The hinges are out of plumb and it takes slow and steady pressure to get the door to shut at all.

Two weeks later, as nice as pie, she calls and invites me to a Ladakhi wedding. I already have an invitation to a Tibetan wedding for that day, but she pleads: the Ladakhi wedding is out in the country, Tenzing cannot go with her, she is uneasy about walking home in the dusk.

So we go to the Ladakhi wedding. For a start I am glad that this gets me out of the Tibetan wedding, for which Dorjee Gyaltsen is in an ecstasy of preparation. He has talked the bride and groom into having a disco tent as well as a beer tent, a gambling tent, a supper tent and a dancing tent. From God knows where he has hired an electricity generator, piles of tapes, three loudspeakers and strings of flashing lights.

While he sets up the disco tent he plays the tapes at full blare. The rocks ring. From five hundred metres away I feel like crawling inside myself to escape the noise. From his office Lobsang Tensing strides towards Dorjee Gyaltsen and his gang of helpers and tells them to cut the racket. It is cruel, he says, to impose that sort of noise on fellow humans. Furthermore, it is an unTibetan noise. Where on earth did they get hold of such trash?

At this criticism of their taste — so Dorjee Gyaltsen tells me over rum — the young men are instantaneously welded into an uprising. They glare defiance at Lobsang Tensing. They tell him you cannot have a wedding these days without a disco tent.

Lobsang Tensing says that in his camp people can get married perfectly well without all that noise. And people will. That is his command.

The young men point at the boundary wall beside the disco tent. The tent is outside the wall. It is beyond the camp. It is, they tell him, beyond his command.

In dread they watch him swing around and stomp back to his office, furious dust rising behind him with every step. He is their leader. Everybody loves him and respects him. And he is no ninny. Their punishment will come at a time of his own choosing. But the day of judgement is safely tucked up in the future and until it comes they nervously mark their victory by playing, louder yet and louder, the shuddering tapes they have hired.

The racket of wedding preparation continues into the night. Next morning I am glad when Astrid and I set off and leave it all behind.

We cross the Choglamsar bridge and follow an upstream track. This is rich country. Here beside the Indus the irrigation channels are full of brisk water. Heavy farmhouses — built two storeys high on top of ground-floor stabling — rise from fields thick with the one forage crop that the brief summer will allow. Across it, rows of bent generations move, grasping handfuls of fodder and mowing it down with sickles. Beyond the irrigation channels, where water cannot reach out to green the desert and the land is fit only for thistles and donkeys, grandmothers too decayed to handle sickles move on walking sticks. Withy baskets on their backs, they patrol the boulders for donkey turds to burn in winter hearths.

Astrid and I, pleasure bent and with ungrimed hands, exclaim at this ideal scene: the earth giving up its harvest, the haymaking families working in unison. They wave and call to us. Like kings and duchesses passing by in carriages, we wave back and approve the happiness simple people derive from their labours.

The wedding itself is in a singularly grand house that I remember from my very first visit to Ladakh. Sonam Batapa, the government cultural officer, had taken me touring with his troupe of dancers and I had found their performance tedious beyond bearing: a series of frozen poses done to the noise of wailing shawms. I had wandered off; the troupe and I lost each other. Children, finding a stranger who uttered incomprehensible noises, led me to the grandest house in the district. The owner, a civil engineer who left the farmwork to others of the family, was home, was fluent in English and went out of his way to reunite the troupe and me.

Now, when Astrid and I enter the great walled garden, festive tents are scattered among the flowers, people in their finest gowns and peraks are drinking chang — and nobody seems to know that Astrid is an invited guest. They take us at her word, though, and at the wedding treasurer's table we hand over the customary wedding present of banknotes in an envelope. The treasurer counts the money and records it in a ledger.

Now we are part of the party. But before we can find a drink someone from the house recognises Astrid. Judged too grand and refined to be part of the common entertainment in the courtyard, we are herded into an upper room where crones and young lamas are seated on the floor. Here we suffer the fate of curates on their parish-visiting rounds: tea and talk and a shared struggle against yawning.

As soon as seems decently possible we walk back down the valley. The disco lights are flashing in the dusk, beery laughter is breaking free from the crash and thump of taped music. We decide, though, against the embarrassment of turning up sober at a party that is well into its stride. So I take Astrid to her door, walk a wide arc around the hooley and head for home.

Candles are burning in the cell next to mine, which is reserved for the camp doctor, who is usually supplied by the French charity Médecins sans Frontières. For months we have been doctorless, but by the look of the light a new one must have arrived.

As I undo my padlock I hear a male voice shout, 'You stupid bitch!' His accent makes bitch sound like beach — another Frenchman, I suppose.

A low soothing females voice follows, but not soothing enough because now the man shouts, 'You bloody stupid bitch!' Between the 'b' and the 'l' of 'bloody' he manages to insert a spare vowel: 'buloody'. Ah, I have it, not French but Australian.

Once I manage to shut the door behind me I hear no more from my new neighbours, only the crash and roar from the wedding disco.

Next morning when I have my new neighbours in for a cup of tea there is no sign of the tensions of the night's shouting. They are Australian doctors, and both make a point of ensuring that I know they are Catholics. During the time we are living side by side he turns out to have a fierce and troubled faith, keen to pick at theological detail, while she takes her religion as something one is born with, just like freckles.

Pam is the daughter of a farming family, Karoly the son of Hungarians who fled the 1956 uprising. They became lovers at medical school and are now on their Wanderjahr. From Sydney they took a Yugoslav plane to Belgrade and went straight to Budapest, where Karoly was under instruction to pray in a side chapel of the cathedral for uncles shot in 1956. Pam's mum had told her to go to some village in England — 'forgotten the bloody name of it now,' she says — where she had to look at gravestones.

'Bloody hundreds of them,' says Karoly.

'Well,' says Pam, 'they'd all lived there since the year dot.'

Trudging through the rain in the graveyard they suddenly realised that, to them, Europe might as well not exist. 'Nothing ever happens there except history,' says Pam. 'And you can never find a shower.' So they hopped on a plane for Bombay and were instantly caught on the updraught of India on the move — crush, colour, jostle, a rush and hunger for tomorrow, filth, inefficiency, charm and naked public curiosity. 'Dear friends,' a stranger on a bus asked them, 'is it true that young Europeans now copulate openly before marriage? And your good selves also?'

In Srinagar they heard about Ladakh and caught the bus to Leh. They arrived yesterday and in the Pamposh Hotel sat next to Carole, the Canadian nurse who helps out at the camp hospital three mornings a week. She brought them here on the late afternoon bus and took them to see Jigme Kunga. Straightaway he offered them unpaid work and the cell next door, whistled up the camp jeep and its driver so they could pick up their packs in town — 'And here we are,' says Pam. 'Isn't it brilliant? Tourists yesterday. And today running the highest hospital in the world.'

'Something for your CV, eh?'

'Shit, yeah,' says Karoly. His expression matches the tone of his voice.

This is Sunday. I have begun to taper off the hunt for the lost lexicographer. So after Pam and Karoly have left to do their hospital rounds, and get used to the idea of having to help hobbling patients walk outside so they can crap on the ground, I force myself into some harsh exercise, a hard march over the river and up to the queen's palace.

Everybody keeps saying that, for five rupees, people can have a look around inside. In the courtyard a yak stands in an open stable. A rope is looped through a willow ring running through its nose and the other end of the rope is knotted to a rafter. I still can't get used to the Ladakhi and Tibetan habit of walking inside without knocking, so I knock and stand by the open door of the palace. No sound comes from inside except for a scratching as if from rats running across a stone floor. But is it not rats, only the Tibetan version of a Pekinese dog. At either end it is so filthy — matted dung and clotted food — that only when it barks am I sure which is fore and which is aft. The barking makes a window above me open. One hand emerges palm down and makes a sideways rocking movement, the why-don't-you-piss-off signal. So I do.

For an hour I walk the downhill zig-zag across boring wilderness and decide I have earned my rum. Dorjee Gyaltsen arrives full of news about the wedding. The disco tent was a roaring success. Never had he seen so much chang. There was even bottled beer from India. From the Kingfisher Brewery, he adds in awe, then turns doubtful as if needing a foreign expert's opinion to support his own: 'This is the best beer, yes?'

I reassure him.

'And after midnight there was many fightings. Kunga-la was bleeding from the nose. And one eye, it was blackened.'

'Gosh, someone'll be in for it. You can't go beating up Kunga-la and get away with it.'

Dorjee Gyaltsen looks surprised. 'But why not? At weddings there are always fightings. It means nothing.'

twelve

The late-afternoon maths tutorials settle down. They started off with fifteen children, and they had to be flexuous children at that because, for a start, they had to sit cross-legged on the floor leaning over their exercise books. My little cell could barely accommodate them, but there was no need to worry. Day by day, numbers dwindled and overcrowding eased.

Now only the hard core remain. Tsering Lhamo — plodding Tsering Lhamo — still attends, her greased face shining, her eyes alight, her brain dragging along behind. Sometimes I watch her eyes scanning my windowpanes and see a frown growing darker at the sight of dirty glass. And every day, as she settles on the floor, she runs a fingertip along the concrete and watches a clean streak appear where her fingertip has moved.

Also a regular is Rigpa Dorjee, the little boy from the back row of desks where he sits hidden among the dunces. I have often wondered about Rigpa Dorjee. Why is he such a runt, and why so slow to learn? Did his family go through famine at a vital age when his brain and his body ought to have been developing at a gallop? Or is he slow because he sits among boys who feel condemned? Has Rigpa Dorjee absorbed their belief that they have no power to shape their own lives? At these rushed tutorials, where he is now one of five instead of one among fifty, his mind clicks and surges ahead.

One of five? Really he is one of seven, but the other two are Dawa Metok and Dorjee Namgyal, and they are not even pretending to be here to take advantage of the extra maths tutoring I am offering.

Dawa Metok arrives alone, without even the pretence of textbook or exercise book, and she sits cross-legged on the floor, saving a space beside her for Dorjee Namgyal. He is always delayed. He is in the top soccer and the top basketball teams, and he has his running training for the school sports next term, so the sportsmaster keeps him back for extra coaching: it is always the brightest apple that gets an extra polish.

Like a princess at a window, Dawa Metok waits while he trains. She tenses at the sound of approaching feet. Her backbone slumps minutely when the wrong person enters her line of vision. Then her face lifts and lights when Dorjee Namgyal leaps from the dust and up on to the concrete platform outside my door. I even feel my own throat clench at the sight of their reunion after — what was it? — an hour apart.

Flushed and glowing from the sportsground, he is leaping about with all the surplus energy of joy. Instead of carefully making his way among the others until he reaches her side, he skips with the accuracy of a chamois among the cross-legged children. Once he even performs a Cossack leap over little Rigpa Dorjee and then sinks to the floor beside Dawa Metok with an exaggerated show of grace as if he were a ballet dancer.

I still do not care for him, though, nor hanker after her. But I envy them. Their lives are fizzing. Even at the cost of having to be young again, I would swap places. They know their love fills the world, that it sweeps and lifts them.

It is, though, only first love. They are so young they cannot even realise that they do not know one another. They have placed the masks of perfection over each other's faces. They are each the invention of the other and they delight in their own inventions. But they are doomed to discover who the other is. And then, at one touch, the tempest could die and dump them on the ground. In twenty years they may struggle to remember one another's names.

Side by side they sit. Like some stiff duenna, I keep glancing to make sure that no parts touch when they tilt their heads towards each other to whisper or to giggle. At every sound from them Tsering Lhamo lowers her brows and shushes them. She still wants to know why negative times positive equals negative, and how can a person discover the answer if other people keep chattering all the time? She has only just quietened them when darkness enters the room. We look up. It is the discipline master standing in the open doorway.

His arrival is like the shadow of a falcon crossing a fowl-run. Movement stops. Bodies shrink. Five faces bent over exercise books swivel up and assume carefully neutral expressions. Even Dawa Metok and Dorjee Namgyal eventually sense the shadow and the silence.

Unlike the others, they are not hunched over work but are sitting upright against the wall, a shade closer together than they might be if mere chance had placed them side by side. At guilty speed they ease apart and stare back at the discipline master. Suddenly their lack of exercise books or textbooks looks as obvious as nudity.

In silence the discipline master returns their stare. Because the lowering sun is behind him we cannot see his expression; we can only see that now he is turning his head towards me. He keeps his grip on the power of silence. And I retain enough self-control to know that if I open my mouth, if I try to explain that I have the headmaster's permission to give these extra maths tutorials, my words will sound defensive, will sound like yammering. He looks back at Dawa Metok and Dorjee Namgyal. Then he is gone as silently as he arrived.

I feel the need to be alone. So I look at my watch. 'Hey, it's getting on. You'd all better hurry home or you'll miss your dinner.' None of the children owns a watch. So they cannot check my shaky lie. When they get to their houses and find they are early perhaps they will think only that the cooks are late this evening.

I wake twitchy. I can see what is going to happen. The discipline master is turning himself into a detective closing in on Dawa Metok and Dorjee

110

Namgyal. So far he has nothing to go on — by my lights they have done nothing except sit together but by the look of the discipline master's visit he has decided to make life unpleasant for them.

Whatever the punishment, Dorjee Namgyal will get by. His success on the sportsfield gives him confidence. But Dawa Metok seems to be still at a teetery stage. She starts at a disadvantage — she is the charity girl, the motherless Ladakhi whom the Tibetans rescued from the rubbish dump and who ought to be grateful. She is moving on from her mother's death. The skin disease that made her hide her face seems to be past. Dorjee Namgyal's attention is bringing her out. But she is — what is she, fourteen, fifteen? — not yet ready for the sort of knockbacks that the discipline master deals in. And if ever he does humble her in front of the school, it will be my fault for letting her and Dorjee Namgyal use my tutorials as a pretext for getting together.

Today I can see no rational solution so I do something irrational. I say, 'Bugger everything. I'm going to take the day off.' Other teachers keep telling me I am silly for not taking a day off whenever I feel like it. All you have to do, they say, is go into the headmaster's office and tell him you have to go into Leh on business and he will say okay.

So here I am sitting on a giant boulder beside the fruitstall the little Kashmiri girl runs and waiting for the morning bus down the valley. In her standard mixture of languages she keeps chucking chatter in my direction. But for the moment it only annoys me. She is saying nothing more than 'Blessings on you . . . Are you well today? . . . Good wishes to you . . . Good morning . . . Hello, hello, hello', which makes me feel that my life here is all pretence and sham, easygoing and amiable on the surface, but underneath no gears are engaging. Life is tedium and emptiness. Life is passing me by. I would be better off at home, inside an office building, under fluorescent lights, with a ballpoint in my hand.

I toss phrases back at her and stare grumpily across the road, where someone from officialdom has put up a roadside hoarding saying 'Erecting Houses Without Authorisation Is Not Permitted', which must be a hint to all of us at the refugee camp, where people are endlessly making sun-dried mud bricks, collecting flat stones and then, with carefully artless expressions on their faces, placing one brick on top of another, sticking them together with wet mud and then standing back in surprise — Hey, look what's happened, a new house for me!

At the base of the hoarding, as if to show that nobody cares for its message, people toss what little rubbish cash-starved lives produce. Now a flock of camp sheep are working their way through our litter. Their muzzles dig down into the junk. One fortunate animal finds a scrap of paper and chews her way through it. Envious for a moment, her sisters give her resentful glances then resume mining among our cast-offs.

Chortens on parade upriver from Tiksey.

From further off comes the pinging of the old people's attempts to buy themselves a good reincarnation. The least ancient inhabitants of the old people's quarter spend their days working for a satisfactory life after death by shuffling around a pilgrims' path that lies on the boundaries of the temple compound. At the corners of the path stand chortens, mud shrines built in the shape of chess pawns. The old people store up merit by walking clockwise from chorten to chorten, by circling each chorten, again clockwise, and by twirling prayer wheels as they walk. As feebleness advances, the aged shorten their daily path. They keep close to the temple walls, shuffling clockwise around and around.

Set in recesses in the outer walls are vertical drums filled with rolled strips of printed prayers. Along the axis of each drum stands an iron rod that allows old fingers to flick the drum into a spin, which activates the paper prayers and, once more, adds to the merit that will be assigned to each soul when its private judgement day arrives and the next incarnations is decided.

Before that day comes, though, one final phase must be passed through. When legs can no longer manage hobbling around the temple walls, the final prayer machine awaits. At the centre of the temple stands a giant prayer wheel, three metres tall and broad in proportion. From the base of the wheel jut spokes that look as if they might have come from the capstan of some sailing ship. Each spoke is strong enough to prop up three or four failing bodies. In their last months old people drape their torsos over the spokes and gently push back on the balls of their feet. Slowly the capstan turns. Inside the drum of the prayer wheel the printed prayers rotate and, with every circuit completed, an arm on top of the drum strikes a bell hanging from the ceiling, which rings a report down to blind prayer-pushers that they have earned another teaspoonful of improved prospects.

This is the pinging I hear as I sit despondent on a roadside boulder, waiting for the bus.

But instead of a bus come two Ladakhi matrons walking in the middle of the road. Each wears across her shoulders a dried goatskin which — or so I guess — serves the same function as a businessman's tie or a Tongan's waistmat: useless symbols of respectability. One woman wears a top hat made of vertically quilted brocade. The proper scoop has been cut out of the front of the brim to bare her forehead. But the other woman's forehead is expensively covered. She wears a perak, an astrakhan wimple with flyaway wings rising above her ears. Running fore and aft across the wimple lies a band of stiffened cloth, the forepart of which is shaped like a cobra's head. On to the cloth is sewn a treasury of turquoise, coral, silver and pearls.

In apathy I track their approach. The two women turn to face me as they walk by. My sour looks must be softening because they grin and call, 'Julay, julay.'

'Julay, julay,' I call back. The fruitstall girl joins in, calling greetings, and all four of us fill the day with our smiles. A good mood is returning like a tide rising and when the two women pass I see good luck approaching — not the squeaky timber-framed bus but a taxi jeep. I raise a hand. Within a hundred metres or so, its brakes manage to get the jeep to a standstill. I run down the road and clamber into the canvas-covered tray.

In a corner sit two Ladakhis. One is a woman in her thirties trying to hold an old man upright. Every other minute she must wrench him back because he has lost all his strength and, if it were not for her, he would slump forward into a heap on the floor. Occasionally his body is racked by spasms of coughing. He only just has the strength to hold on to an empty tin on his lap. From his lips to the rim of the tin hangs a string of phlegm. And every time he coughs beads of blood escape from his lips and slide down the slime.

We are all too busy now to fret about the discipline master. It's the end of term, and holidays are coming, but first we have to buy our vacation with exams. So kids who have been slacking their way through the term feel jolts of fear and rush the extra maths tutorials.

I try to prepare a fair examination paper but give in to one temptation: I include a question that steps outside the syllabus. To get the answer will require no special knowledge but it will test simple logic. Once I have put in the question I am seized by worry over my honesty. Am I being straight with the kids? Do students with an inborn ability deserve a bonus mark over earnest students who have to work hard? Such a dainty conscience! In the end I leave the question in but put it at the end of the paper. That way, slow children will not get stuck on it and waste time that could better have been spent on questions which fall within the syllabus.

It turns out that only Sonam Dakpa and Dawa Metok get the answer to it. Sonam Dakpa's success is no surprise. That aloof little boy has never slipped from his place at top of the class. And he has never given me a chance to relax. In class his brain keeps pace step by step with mine. The difference, though, is that I have had to take hours every night going over tomorrow's lesson until I think I understand it well enough to spout it back to the class. But every morning, within minutes of opening my mouth, Sonam Dakpa is in command of every angle that it took me all night to grasp.

I feel specially happy at Dawa Metok's correct answer. And depressed. What sort of life is there for bright kids like her living up here in one small unknown fold of this immense mountain range? By the standards of what other people here experience, she may have a perfectly satisfactory life. I don't go along with the notion that the plodding blinkered peasant life of struggling just to avoid starvation is more satisfying than sitting behind a computer terminal getting rich by currency trading, but there is no fairness in letting a small proportion of the world hog all advantages at the cost of denying them to the majority.

Not that my fifty VA refugees show any sign, when I hand back their exam papers, of allowing anything to hold them down.

Sonam Dakpa, like a rich man opening the envelope that has brought him another dividend cheque, glances quickly to make sure I have got my own arithmetic right — a ninety-five per cent pass — and then folds the paper away, not even a flicker of satisfaction at the ends of his lips.

Half the other children, though, explode in protest at my marking. It is my own fault that I set off this protest. Once I have handed back all their papers, I go to the blackboard and ignite their indignation by showing how the questions should have been worked out. When I finish Karma Yeshi rises from his place near the wall, clambers up on to the seat of his chair and goes through the routine of shoving aside the bottoms of other children so that he can climb along the row of chairs, jump down into the aisle and face me. He has organised his face into a blend of charm, confidence and dismay at my negligence.

'Sir,' he says, 'all my answers I got right. But you have marked so many of them wrong'.

He hands me his exam paper as proof. And he seems to be right. Every answer is correct.

'Your markings are not proper,' he announces, and then pauses before adding on a sly and baiting note: 'Sir.'

I stare at his answers. Why on earth have I put beside them the big bold crosses I scrawl near every wrong answer? I begin to prepare my mouth for a stuttery apology. But then I notice. Every correct answer marked with a cross is written on an area of roughened paper. When I was showing the class how the questions should have been answered, was Karma Yeshi gently at work with a razorblade, lightly scuffing away the surface of the paper until his wrong answers disappeared? And then did he copy the right answers from my blackboard examples?

As I stare, Karma Yeshi must be studying my expression. He must be convincing himself that I am dismayed at my carelessness because now, in lilting confidence, he asks, 'See, I am the best boy in the class, no?'

'Karma Yeshi,' I reply, 'I think you and I both know how these answers got here.'

He bounces back. 'It is because you have taught me so well, sir. I always think you are the best teacher I have ever had.'

But now the words are too confident, as if even Karma Yeshi knows he is overplaying a hopeless hand. He looks at me more closely. At last I can see that he is beginning to read my expression properly. So he clasps his hands and raises them imploringly. He lets his left knee ease forward and he tips his torso leftwards. With the knee no longer supporting his weight fully, his body falls sideways and, in a great display of self-control, he resists the instinct to throw out a hand to break his fall. Instead he hits the floor, with both hands still in the attitude of prayer.

Lying down, he implores me, 'Oh, sir, do not thrash me. I am a poor boy. I need the best marks. I must make my own way in the world.'

'Stand up, boy.'

He needs a prod with my toe and threats of worse to come before he will stop his play-acting and get on his feet again.

'Karma Yeshi, I think you will make your way very well indeed, with or without good marks. Either that, or prison.'

He beams back at me, ignoring my final words. His pointy teeth glisten. 'Oh, thank you. Thank you, sir.'

As he clambers back to his proper place, I am rushed by other pupils, their voices clattering with demands that I correct my own marking mistakes. Some have simply crossed out the wrong answers and copied the right answers. Some have gone in for crude forgery, overprinting the correct answer on top of the wrong. Others, in their rough haste to scratch away their mistakes, have ripped holes in their papers.

The school bell rings. End of lesson. End of day. End of exams. End of term. Tomorrow the school truck will take my VA kids back on holiday to their family tents up on the heights of Jhun Thang — all except Sonam Dakpa and Dawa Metok.

He, with his ninety-five per cent pass in his pocket, will cross the road into Choglamsar village to be with his widowed mother.

And Dawa Metok will walk down the valley into Leh where, in the low-ceilinged stable in the rubbish dump beside the palace, she will spend two weeks being housekeeper for her father and her monkish brother.

As for me, I am going walking in the hills.

thirteen

Going walking in the hills was no sudden decision. It must be more than a year ago that I asked the Survey of India for large-scale maps of Ladakh. Their reply looked as if it had been written by someone trying to take the mickey out of Indian bureaucracy. No, said the Survey of India, I could not buy any maps of Ladakh. How could any responsible government department sell maps of such a sensitive area?

But if I could persuade the head of a diplomatic mission in New Delhi to vouch for me, the Survey of India would gladly sell him the maps I wanted and he could resell them to me on the understanding that he and I would, jointly and severally, be responsible for my complying with the conditions of sale, viz:

1(a) I must place myself under the jurisdiction of the Indian courts.

  (b) I must promise that if ever I was charged with an offence under the Indian Official Secrets Act I would appear in person in court to answer the charge(s).

2(a) I must promise, if ever I was allowed a map, never to show it to anyone.

  (b) I must promise to keep any maps under lock and key.

  (c) I must promise every year to file a return to the Survey of India attesting that I still had the map, that I kept it constantly under lock and key and had never shown it to anybody.

3(a) I must promise that, if ever an officer of the Indian military or an Indian forest ranger demanded that I surrender the map, I would promptly hand it over.

(b) I must also undertake that when, after long use, the map became illegible or otherwise unserviceable, I would return it at my own expense to the Survey of India for destruction.

(c) I must finally undertake that, if I surrendered the map to a military officer or a forest ranger in response to his lawful demand, I must not sue or attempt to sue any branch or department of the Indian government for compensation or any other form or style of recompense whatsoever.

(d) No such attempt to claim compensation or recompense would be recognised or entertained by the government of India.

4(a) All applicants wishing to buy a Survey of India map must complete the portion of the official application form and state therein whether they wish to buy a plain unmounted map or a varnished map mounted on a wall roller suitable for classroom use or public display.

I gloated at being the owner of the Survey of India's reply and was tempted to write to all the ambassadors in New Delhi to see whether any of them would sponsor my attempt to buy a map. But somehow I discovered the Survey of India and the United States Defense Department shared copyright in the maps I needed, so I wrote to the Pentagon and got a more forthright answer: We sell no maps to aliens.

Now I rang the librarian at the geography department of our local university and asked what map agent she dealt with. She gave me the address of a shop in England and, within two weeks, the maps arrived in my letterbox. They were not the crisp engravings I had hoped for but only fuzzy photocopies, not that a bit of fuzziness mattered greatly. The maps were sixty years out of date and a note in the margins said that their accuracy could not be guaranteed: in fact, if any user noticed any mistakes the Defense Department would be grateful if a corrected copy of the map could be sent to the Pentagon, which would promptly send a free replacement copy of the original unreliable map.

By the time I reached Bombay and set off northwards towards the refugee camp, I had almost memorised one of the maps, and by the time I put on my backpack and set off from the camp on my walking holiday I had plotted every step I would take, and somehow my mind had pushed aside the clear message the map was giving: I was dotty even to think of walking where I planned to go.

Over the first few days the route I had chosen would take me into the uninhabited head of a valley, where I would face a 4500-metre pass. I knew that, around 4000 metres, my climbing slowed to a shuffle even if I had nothing more than a daypack on my back. But by the time I reached the pass I would have a full-size pack laden with clothes, a sleeping bag, a scrap of a tent and food for several days.

If I managed to get over the pass, a donkey track would lead the way down another valley with only three hamlets in it. Then, three days after crossing the pass, the track would end on the banks of the Zanskar River, a muscular torrent of silt which, at that point, roared deep down inside unscalable cliffs.

Sixty years ago, when the map was drawn, a rope swingbridge crossed the Zanskar at the point to which I planned to walk. I knew that rope bridges in the Zanskar Valley were made by twisting twigs together and that, when new, they were usually strong enough to carry one person at a time. But what might I find there now? The rotting ends of broken ropes dangling into a canyon? And what then?

With two days' food remaining, I could turn around and try to retrace a six-day walk. Or I could turn left and try to reach the point where the Zanskar empties into the Indus. There I could turn left again and see if I could follow the Indus down to Alchi, a village of enchanting twelfth-century temples plus a modern steel bridge that would get me back to the sealed Srinagar-Leh road.

Walking to Alchi would be shorter but far riskier. If I turned back, at least I would know that there was a track all the way to my starting point. But from the Zanskar gorge to Alchi the map showed no track nor any reason for a track. There was no sign on the map of a hamlet, farmhouse or even a shepherd's summer shelter. And with my own eyes I had seen the land from a distance: violently crumpled rock with no creeks and therefore nowhere to refill my water bottles. Usually I reckon myself to be on the timorous side of cautious. So why was I now studying the map, seeing the dangers — and shrugging?

Jigme Kunga, though, did his best to warn me of a danger I had not even considered. Wolves. If I saw a pack of them on the move, he enquired, did I know that it was foolish to get in front of them and try to bar their way? And if I was at the mouth of a rocky indentation inside which a pack of wolves had gathered, did I know that they would get jumpy if I stood there because they hated to feel corralled and might respond by eating me?

I promised not to be bossy with wolf packs. Even so, he still farewelled me in a manner that suggested I was being inconsiderate, because how could I expect him to find a quick replacement for me when I failed to return?

In Leh I catch the bus to Lamayuru, the dizzyingly lovely village that rides a cliff of clay just below the crest of Photu La, a 4000-metre pass on the road back to the Vale of Kashmir.

The bus stops beside a track that runs down to Lamayuru, and seven other people get out with me: three nurses from Paris, their medical student boyfriends and a holy man who is following the Hindu tradition of leaving his family and spending his final years as a beggar in search of the final truth.

This particular holy man is no humble seeker. At one stage I ask him, 'Are you looking for God?' and he replies snappishly, 'No, God is looking for me.'

121

In Ladakh he has been inspecting Buddhism and finding it unsatisfactory. Before that he had visited a sacred cave on the southern slopes of the Great Himalayan Range, a cave to which Hindu pilgrims walk in their thousands to adore a stalagmite that they believe was placed there by the heavenly powers to remind the faithful of the forces inside an erect penis. The holy man now writes off the trip to the stalagmite as a waste. He is an educated man, he tells me, and he cannot be bothered with the childish myths of ignorant priests.

But, while walking back through pine forests after visiting the stalagmite, he met another holy man who was living, like a cross-legged statue, beneath a tree. He himself joined the other holy man and for a few weeks they sat together — two grandfathers who had run away from home — waiting to see if the heart of the matter would be revealed to them. No. It was not.

Dragonsback ridges surround tiny barley terraces at Lamayuru.

'But that other man, he taught me a skill I am still not comprehending. He showed me how to control my own body heat. At night we sat in snow and we felt no cold.'

Here the holy man waved a hand to indicate the French and me. 'Just look at you,' he commanded. 'Look at the mighty packs upon your backs. Inside you have woollen underwear, is it not true? And in your great cities you bought sleeping bags for your brave expedition. True or false? And now, by way of comparison, look at what I carry.'

He holds a hand out to show more clearly the bundle he carries wrapped in a strip of cotton. It is the size of his skull. 'This is all I own. I sleep on stones under stars. My body is nearly naked — a half-naked fakir.'

With that phrase — Churchill's description of Gandhi — contempt enters his voice. 'And you with your great wealth will sleep tonight in a hotel bed. You will be covered in clothes and wrapped in sleeping bags. I am right, am I not?'

At this point we are halfway down the track that runs from the road to Lamayuru village. Ahead the bulk of the monastery rears up above a forest of chortens. To our right a broad wall of stones spills down the hillside. It is a mani wall and its only function is to hold up to heaven the thousands of flat stones that pave its upper surface, each stone carved with the Tibetan letters for 'Om mani padme hum' — Hail to the jewel in the lotus blossom. Here, beside the mani wall, also stands a sign:

YUNG DUNG HOTEL
T. Norbu, Prop.

On the board an arrow points to the right. I know the Yung Dung, so automatically I veer right and grasp my walking stick in front of me to act as a third leg that will stop me from tipping over as the track plunges downhill.

The others slither behind me. We pass the Lamayuru shop and post office (locked as usual), the village spring, the row of lombardy poplars beside it, the village school with its motto painted in English over the front door — 'Many Mrickles Make a Muckle' (Yes, yes, it says mrickles) — then finally we stand outside the Yung Dung, where Mr Norbu grabs my elbows and grins into my face. To the French and the holy man he makes an announcement: 'My friend has come back.'

Mr Norbu's hotel has grown mightily since my first walking holiday. Then it was a simple single-storeyed building of mud bricks, furnished only with iron-framed beds that looked as if they had once fallen off the back of an army truck. He also had one steel table, which guests lugged from room to room depending on where they wished to dine, and a few folding steel chairs.

In those days a notched poplar trunk leaned against the hotel to act as a ladder for a Muslim father and his sons, who were camped on the flat roof and lackadaisically building an extra storey for Mr Norbu. They ate on the roof and slept on the roof and, when they went to sleep, they cocooned their entire bodies in sheets, their heads completely covered so that, even quite late in the morning when the sun had left Tibet and was well established in the sky, the still-sleeping builders were a colony of caterpillars reluctant to pupate and start the day's work.

But now their work was completed and on the upper floor a cluster of cells provided private bedrooms. 'One for each person,' boasted Mr Norbu.

To my mind, the improvements detracted from the Yung Dung. Previously when you went to bed in the large ground-floor rooms there was no knowing whom you might wake with. Mr Norbu did not lock his doors, so travellers who found their way to the Yung Dung during the night would step inside and, on tiptoe, fumble and flail, while feeling each bed to see which was empty. Then would come the sound of boots being dumped on the floor, the slithery noise of a sleeping bag emerging from a pack and being filled with a body, the creak of a bed accepting the weight of Mr Norbu's newest guest and, finally, the groany sigh of a traveller who had found a bed and a roof.

Although Mr Norbu had expanded his hotel, he still clung to his open-air lavatory in the hotel yard. The Muslim builders, who had dug a pit from which to extract the clay for their sun-dried bricks, immediately gave the pit an extra function by converting it into a self-cleaning lavatory. Urine moistened the clay and made it malleable, and their daily turds were blended in with the mud when they were moulding a fresh supply of bricks. Hotel guests followed the builders' lead, jetting their urine into the pit or crouching on its rim. It all added to the sense of having stepped outside the Sheraton world. Today, though, with the bricks made and the builders gone, the pit is no longer self-emptying, and the contributions to it have multiplied. By the look and the smell, Mr Norbu's Yung Dung Hotel is a great commercial success.

But prosperity has not changed Mr Norbu. He is still an uninspired cook. Rice, dhal, fried eggs and greasy pancakes of flour and water are still all that he can manage. When the holy man, the French and I take our places around the steel dining table, the holy man heaps rice and dhal on to one of Mr Norbu's tin plates while the rest of us sit back and stare at the food.

Mr Norbu, crouched in the corner over his kerosene pressure-stove, rises and brings over a pan paved with eggs fried crinkly-brown. He has a rubbery face that flickers all day between delight and misery. Seeing our reluctance to eat, his face goes hangdog. We respond by applying dainty portions to our plates. He applies one fried egg to each dob of rice and dhal.

From his white beard the holy man brushes rice on to the table and observes us closely. 'Please let me make one observation. Each of you is breathing wrongly. Pray observe my breathing.'

We watch. He patrols our eyes.

'Ugh! You are not understanding. You cannot see. You strain to breathe in. I put all my efforts into breathing out. Your way stores waste. It tantamounts to using your body as a coffin for putrefaction. Yes, a coffin. But my way cleanses the body. I eject waste. Now, please, under my instructions, please follow me.'

He mouth-breathes so that he can call the count for breathing in and breathing out. The French medical student who seems to be the leader of the group takes a packed of Panama cigarettes from a pocket, lights up and directs a fine jet of smoke at the holy man. With elaborate politeness he asks, in English, 'Pray, sir, what are your qualifications for this lecture?'

The holy man switches to French and says that he took his medical degree in France, at Lyons as a matter of fact. The French freeze.

The holy man savours the silence, and when he has had enough, he returns to English. 'I am only a simple homeopath . . .'

The smoking student rolls his eyes to the ceiling. 'Homeopathy! A charlatan. I should have guessed it.'

'Do not apologise for your envy and your anger,' says the holy man. 'All my life I am knowing envy. In Varanasi my practice grew so famous. I made much money. I published widely in all the professional journals.' His voice jumps when he repeats the phrase 'all the professional journals. My standing, it was so great that enemies whispered and plotted.'

But his words are now overwhelmed by a tide of argument among the French. The smoking student tells his friends to ignore the charlatan; there is nothing to learn from paranoid ravings. The others disagree. They find the symptoms interesting to observe. I am looking from French face to French face, trying to catch the words. When I give up the effort the holy man has disappeared.

He reappears at breakfast and is disinclined to talk.

'Where did you sleep, Babu?' I ask.

'Outside,' he replies, so gruffly that I suspect he thinks I doubt his claim to sleep on stones.

But suddenly he turns bubbly and enthusiastic and talks about the other holy man who taught him how to slow his heartbeat when he felt too hot and to speed it when cold.

'Do you know why I left that man? It was because I could not stand the nights. It was not the snow, it was the noises. Not at all could I tolerate sitting under that man's tree hearing wild beasts howling and walking close by.' He laughs at the absurdity of it all. 'I learn how to make my mind control my body. But my mind cannot control itself. All those nights I nearly cried with fear.'

I am willing to sit and listen to him forever, or at least until the French get up and start baiting him, because I am in a nervy state. I am itching to start my walk but at the same time I have been casting about for an excuse — any excuse — for delay: excited at the prospect, nervous of the outcome.

While the holy man talks, a spare part of my brain adopts a delaying tactic that will provide a good day's walk but still get me back to the familiar safety of the Yung Dung by nightfall. I shall walk down a gorge that used to terrify nineteenth-century travellers. Then I'll go on to look at a bridge that early kings of Ladakh used as part of a trap in which they forced traders to hand over money. From there I'll carry on and get lunch at a village called Khalse. That's where the Dalai Lama's junior tutor's reincarnation has been born, an enchanting village in summer because it stretches along an avenue of walnut trees, so its teastalls are shaded and made pungent by the spicy smell falling from walnut leaves above. Then I'll hurry back to Lamayuru for dinner and make an early start tomorrow.

European travellers hated the gorge that I want to see because it is so narrow and its walls are so sheer that there is no natural pathway through it. But it lay across a minor byway of the old silk road and, to ease trade, the Ladakhis somehow drove spikes into the cliffs that line the gorge and upon the spikes they laid planks, with gaping spaces between them. Occasionally one plank had to be lower than its neighbours, and for travellers it was a moment of terror when, balancing on one of those lofty planks, they had to urge trembling horses to step across the void and the drop where the levels changed.

I, though, expect the gorge to be a doddle because, in the descriptions of European travellers, the horrors of the gorge grow milder with the passing years.

The first Englishman to pass through was a veterinary surgeon called George Moorcroft, who used to annoy his employers, the East India Company. From Calcutta his boss once wrote complaining that, instead of looking after company horses, he was forever 'rambling about the country on wild and romantic excursions'. Moorcroft disliked the gorge intensely but he was in a jumpy mood anyway. A few days before, one of his horses had slipped while going through Wolf's Leap Gorge. It was the very horse that was carrying his folding brass bedstead and, when the horse stumbled, Moorcroft saw his bed slide off and fall into the crushing rush of the Dras River. So wild is the water that it was pointless to think of rescue and, anyway, the folding brass bedstead would have been crumpled within seconds.

Those were the days of heroic travel — and of strings of even more heroic servants, horses and mules tottering under the weight of equipment

Dawn strips the coverings of night from Lamayuru.

that their masters thought would be necessary in the wilderness. A later Englishman made his caravan of men and beasts carry a 'folding leathern bath', and Sven Hedin, whose travels made him a national hero in Sweden, included among his equipment a folding sailing boat. This, he thought, would ease travel through Tibet: on board his fleet craft he would demolish the tedious miles as he skimmed lightly over Tibetan lakes.

But in the end, Hedin had to admit it was a theory that sounded fine in Stockholm but silly in Tibet. As his boat approached the farther shore of his first lake, he noticed a pack of wolves waiting for him. Not wanting to become their lunch, he picked a fresh landing point. But the wolves sidled around the shore and gathered at his new destination. The game went on and on and by the time he had made a safe landfall Hedin had given away the idea of Tibet as a place to go sailing.

Theodore Roosevelt Jnr and Kermit Roosevelt, sons of President Theodore Roosevelt, carried somewhere in their baggage dinner jackets, boiled shirts and black ties in case they met any local kings who might invite them to share a meal. For reading they had *Mr Midshipman Easy,* and beside them ran cougar hounds, the gift of Mr Bob Bakker of Montana.

Sir Francis Younghusband, though, was a light traveller — and a lighter traveller than he wished. By the time he reached the gorge near Lamayuru, he had been seven months on the road, walking from Beijing on an expedition to discover passes which the Russians might use if ever they decided to spill over the Karakoram mountains and try to drive the British out of India.

Dressed in a Central Asian gown and carrying a pickaxe and a bottle of brandy, he travelled by way of the Gobi and the Zungaria deserts and, after finding no passes through which the Czar's armies could flood, he made his way over the mountains, using his pickaxe as an alpenstock. Coming down one near-vertical patch of ice, he felt a movement inside the pouch of his gown and heard a tinkling below. It was the brandy bottle sprinkling its entire contents over the mountain. He had promised himself that he would not succumb to temptation and pull the cork until he had reached land over which flew the Union Jack.

And then, when he got down into Ladakh, he found a Russian who had already reached India. The man was called Notovitch and he had been living upstream from Leh at Hemis Monastery, where he claimed to have found documents proving that Christ had survived the cross, had hobbled across Persia, through India, over the Himalayas and up to Hemis. For Notovitch, this was to turn out to be a profitable discovery; later he moved on to America, where he made a living on the lecture circuit, talking about Christ's post-crucifixion adventures.

The story is still a money-spinner in Srinagar, where Christ is supposed to have settled down and married after his visit to Hemis. People in Srinagar who claim to be Christ's descendants own a mausoleum outside a repairing tailor's shop and hang a tin by the door into which visitors drop money before entering the mausoleum and wondering which of two raised slabs they are supposed to venerate.

Younghusband met Notovitch on the track to Srinagar and, although Younghusband was put out that Notovitch was not English, he passed the time of day with him civilly enough, even though he grew more and more convinced that Notovitch was a bounder. On parting, Notovitch went further down in Younghusband's estimation. By comparison with Younghusband, the Russian had barely scratched the fringes of Central Asia yet he had the impertinence to strike a theatrical pose and utter the words: 'We part here, pioneers of the East.'

The latest news of the fearful gorge is dated 1904, when Jane E. Duncan passed through. Miss Duncan was the sickly motherless child of a Glasgow ironmaster. She led a mild and enclosed life until her father and her aunt died and she became free to shuck off her frailties and start living. She was then fifty-two.

In Vancouver she persuaded an engine-driver — a fellow Scot — to bolt a seat on to the cow-catcher of his locomotive so that she could get the best possible view when travelling through the Rockies. On horseback she rode from Jerusalem to Damascus. Japan. Morocco, Nepal, Uganda

— on her own she visited them all. And she took a summer off to take a look at Western Tibet. When she approached the terrifying gorge she wondered how her nerves would handle it. But by then the airy planks were gone. Instead more than twenty bridges lay across the stream to make an easy path along the bed of the gorge.

For me, the gorge turns out to be even easier. Instead of having so many bridges to maintain, the people have piled rock upon rock as the base of a pathway that clings to the cliff. In parts the path is narrow and high, but it feels more secure than any gallery balanced on spikes.

There are two puzzles along the way, though: a mess of wild rhubarb lying on the path and a small stone I spot with a convoluted surface. The first puzzle resolves itself when I overtake a man and his daughter driving a train of donkeys loaded with rhubarb, the second when I roll the stone in my hand and recognise what it is — fossilised brain-coral from the days when the Himalayas were part of the Indian Ocean seabed.

The track reaches the main road and soon I am staring at the bridge and the ruins of the customs trap that the king built at a point where another and more formidable gorge slices a twenty-metre gap out of the road. Here the king made his men throw a cantilevered bridge of poplar trunks across the gorge. Then, hard up against the bridge, he built an inviting guesthouse.

Traders heading for the main strands of the old silk road had a choice: they could gamble on getting themselves and their beasts down an appalling track to the base of the gorge, or they could stroll across the bridge and get a meal or a bed in the guesthouse that straddled the bridge approach. But the people who made the obvious choice discovered that, as soon as they had driven their beasts into the courtyard, the king's men would lock the gate behind them. They were prisoners until they paid for the opposite gate to be opened.

Today the poplar trunks of the king's bridge remain and a few planks still lie athwart them. Even now a tightrope artist might still manage to get over. But walking across would be pure show-off because the army has built a steel bridge nearby to carry its convoys of war supplies up towards the Chinese border.

A sentry-box stands beside the bridge. Here the road is perilously close to the border with Pakistan — another armed and jumpy frontier. Anyone straying from the tarseal will set the hills crackling and pinging with gunshot and ricochet. In India and Pakistan anybody photographing any bridge is likely to be arrested. But I assure myself that the king's old bridge must be an exception. I am taking a few shots of it when I grow aware of someone standing beside me. He wears the uniform of an Indian army private. In his hands he grasps a rifle. The bayonet is fixed. Its tip is pointing at my waist. I try a friendly, 'Oh, hello there. I didn't notice you', but he says nothing. He looks unamused.

With a nod of his head he directs me to the sentry-box. I decide this is a good time for calmness and, at as leisurely a pace as I can manage, I stow the camera, hoist my pack on to my back and walk to the army bridge. Our approach is covered by a man in sergeant's uniform. He, too, is armed and unchatty. He points me upstream towards Khalse and off I stroll, pretending not to notice that the private is behind me, presumably with his bayonet at my back. From the bridge we climb to flat land, where I put on a brisk pace and keep up the pretence that I am the only person moving across this patch of barrenness where close hills concentrate the sun's heat. The outrider poplars, the walnut and apricot trees of Khalse and the first teastall appear. Still not turning around, I swerve off to the teastall. I am, damn it, parched.

But the soldier makes a barking noise. I turn and put on an expression that is supposed to say: 'My dear chap, you haven't been walking all this way with me, have you?' His reply comes from the tip of his bayonet. He flicks it towards the main part of Khalse. And I obey. Into a grove of apricots he herds me. We come to a stop outside the padlocked door of the police station. The time is 12.13. The police must be out for lunch. I drop my pack, pull out some food and offer the private some. The poor man is tempted, but he stands at attention and stares past me. I sit, lean against my pack and chew.

Sharing the shade of the apricot trees are three carpenters. With adzes and drawknives they have been stripping and squaring poplar trunks. But now they also are sitting on the ground and relaxing over food. They keep calling to the soldier with questions that seem to be teasing. He remains stiff and silent. They wander over and inspect me. One bends to look more closely. 'Chinese spy?' he asks. He turns his question back into Ladakhi and the other two laugh. Now he gives the soldier's shoulder a playful shove and the three of them urge him to have a cup of tea with them. The soldier's body deflates. He walks over to the carpenters' workplace, only fifty metres away and well within shooting range. They fall into easy chatter.

A naughty thought enters my head. I take out my camera and, shielding it behind my pack, I unload and reload it. The exposed film gets pushed to the bottom of the pack.

A spacious hour passes. A police sub-inspector strolls back from lunch and unlocks the station. He is a man who has moulded himself to the Indian officer-class pattern: a solemn caricature of a posh 1930s Englishman. 'My dear fellow, I haven't kept you waiting, have I?' He apologises for the way I have been forced to appear before him. 'Those military chaps are quite bonkers about their blessed bridges.'

I break open my camera and feel pleased with the grand gestures I am making. In front of his eyes I am unreeling the film. It turns a milky khaki. With elaborate courtesy, I hand it over to him.

He looks grateful. He can recognise a gentleman when he sees one. I have saved him the embarrassment of having to go through a chap's private possessions and forcibly destroy his film. To demonstrate that all this unpleasantness is over, he tosses the film into his wastepaper basket and says, 'Now I really must give you a cup of tea.'

I hesitate. I have tricked him. I cannot now accept his hospitality.

So we shake hands. We bow. We give cries of pleasure at having had the honour of meeting one another. I hoist my pack, go to a teastall, then hurry back to Lamayuru, where the Yung Dung is deserted. Worse, the ever-open doors are bolted and padlocked.

Where can Mr Norbu be?

fourteen

Mr Norbu is at the village spring. With him are five donkeys and ten jerrycans. He is marvellously drunk and is having trouble. The jerrycans do not want to stand at the point where the spring water will fall into them. And when he does manage to swing a full jerrycan on to a donkey's back, he cannot get the handle of the can to fit over one of the hooks on either side of the saddle.

A group of women waiting to fill their own jerrycans are mocking him. He turns on them and lets loose a speech that is both spluttery and eloquent. Their backs straighten, their heads rise, their faces turn indignant. They hector him.

He notices me. 'My good friend,' he calls. His voice has taken on a cadgy edge. 'Once again you are come back.'

I sense the real message behind his words: he would welcome help. My hands are steadier than his. Together we work smoothly and soon we are on our way uphill with the five laden donkeys. But we are moving away from the Yung Dung and along an empty ridge above the village. I am too puffed to ask why. And, anyway, Mr Norbu is deep in song.

One minute we are on desolate slopes, the next we are standing on a patch of flat ground beside an army dugout. The soldiers are drunker than Mr Norbu. They wave arms, shout and welcome us with cups of rum.

All come from Karnataka, far away in the balmy south. This is their last night of a hateful tour of duty. One grabs my shoulders and, grinning, shouts at me, 'Ladakh is arseholes.' Tomorrow they will all be strolling the avenues of Bangalore with a night breeze moving the boughs and leaves above them, with people all around on the footpaths and lighted shops lining their way. But this evening they are getting rid of their rum rations.

The dugout is large and littered with beds. One door opens on to the flat patch where Mr Norbu and I arrived. Along the outer edge of the flat ground lies a parapet of sandbags. On the far side of the sandbags a ravine falls down and disappears in the gathering gloom.

Here Mr Norbu starts a dance that looks as if it ought to be performed on the spot. Instead, with a horrible inevitability, Mr Norbu starts moving towards the sandbags and the ravine. The sandbags are below the point of balance on a man's body. If Mr Norbu staggers into them suddenly there could be no Mr Norbu, only a fading gargling cry as he disappears overboard. The sergeant rushes to draw him back. Mr Norbu fights free, throws himself at the sandbags, drapes his body over them and goes into spasms of vomiting. The soldiers cheer and pour more rum.

A Ladakhi boy who seems to be employed by the soldiers has unloaded the donkeys. So the sergeant transfers Mr Norbu's body to a donkey's back and makes clicking noises with his tongue. The donkeys obey and, in line astern, they pick their way downhill. In Mr Norbu's draped body the only sign of life is that his hands are clasped firmly around the donkey's neck. 'That way the man is safer,' says the sergeant.

We all move into the dugout and start serious drinking, except for the sergeant. He must keep India safe through the night. So he goes to a radio-telephone on the wall and begins to intone: 'Hello, Khalse. Hello, Khalse. Hello, Khalse.' No response. He shrugs and fills a cup. Through the night he repeats the process. Never does Khalse answer. But the sergeant has done his duty. If an endless convoy of Chinese tanks, troop trucks and officers' jeeps is rolling down the road to Srinagar, so be it. He logs each call to prove that it was not his fault.

From the kitchen the Ladakhi boy appears with two live chickens in his hands. A Buddhist, he cannot kill them himself. Neither can Hindu soldiers. But one soldier rises without being asked, opens his pocketknife and slices neat incisions in the fowls' necks. The boy drops them on the mud floor to jiggle and writhe. Folding his pocketknife, the soldier turns to me. 'See? I am their Catholic,' he explains.

We are awash with rum and getting more so. Now all the dugout team make me their father confessor and take it in turns to explain why they loathe Ladakh. For three years they have been stuck in their dugout. Whichever way they look there is no sign of human life, no tree, no grass. If they walk down to Lamayuru, the people look the other way. In Khalse the people stare at them as if they were insects. Apart from people paid to bring water and food, I am their first visitor.

Three years, three winters. It is inhuman, they say, to send Indian troops into the horrors of these mountains in winter. The men are specially sour about the door to the dugout. There is a gap of about 300 millimetres between the threshold and the bottom of the door. Can I imagine, they ask, the frozen draught that comes roaring through the gap? I look sympathetic but hold my tongue. What I cannot imagine is the weight of misery that has allowed them to spend three years here without raising the threshold or plugging the gap to keep the draught out.

Around eleven o'clock the boy appears with rice and curried chicken. In three minutes flat it has disappeared, we have tossed our tin plates on to the floor and have collapsed on beds.

It is still dark when I start working my way down the ridge from the dugout towards Lamayuru. I shall never be here again, in the village that over the years has filled my eyes with love, and when I say goodbye I want to be seeing Lamayuru at its best.

By the time I pass the spring, a faint line of light lies along the snaggled mountaintops. The sun is lifting itself out of Tibet. In the barley fields

Other travellers near Lamayuru.

beyond the Yung Dung, irrigation rills catch the light and define the footpaths through the crops. I cross the stream and climb a slope of slate. This is old seabed mud, compressed by the weight of the Indian Ocean and still bearing the impress of seaweed. Frost-crumbled, the slate slips downhill under my weight. It takes two paces to climb one step but by the time darkness has turned to a general gloom I am established on a ledge where I sit — an old voyeur — and watch daylight strip the night coverings from Lamayuru.

And here comes the moment. The first pink shaft touches the highest ridges and, turning gold, comes sliding down, stroking the thighs of the mountains, gliding over the nipple-tipped chortens around the monastery and flooding green barley fields that glare against a backdrop of desert.

Below the monastery, a vertically gilled mudstone cliff is set with empty eye-sockets: caves where sealed-in hermits lived, hoping to earn their tickets to Nirvana. By way of contrast, houses limpeted to rock slopes below the cliffs hold glowing faces out to the light. To the right the new sun plays among steeples and towers left behind on the shoreline when a lake drained and disappeared — the same lake where a holy man once threw crumbs to the lake spirit and was blessed when the spirit emerged and drew the sign of the yung dung on a beach.

I stand. I have seen Lamayuru emerge and now I have kilometres and heights to cover. Down I slither and find the track that, in six days, may lead me to the Zanskar ravine, where I shall discover whether a rope swingbridge still offers a way of escaping the unvisited valleys I want to see.

The start is still familiar ground: a track the width of my boots has been chipped into a cliff-face and leads to a side valley where the going is easy. Then the way swings left to a puffing ascent of Prinkiti La. (As well as being a male honorific, 'la' can mean pass, as in Shangri La.)

Resting on the crest of the pass, I watch the approach of a string of donkeys driven by two women. The final donkey bears a child, perhaps two years old, fast asleep and stretched along the animal's spine. Its hands cling to the girth strap and stop it sliding down over the donkey's rump. The donkey crosses the ridge of Prinkiti La. Its back tips over and now slopes downhill. Still asleep, the infant adjusts by bracing its elbows so that it is pushing against gravity. The women pass. Once more I am alone.

I sit a while, staring at the horrorscape that lies ahead. Immediately in front a zig-zag path falls into a ravine, behind the far slope of which stand row upon row of mountain ridges looking like a hundred scenery flats propped against a wall in a theatre basement. I can see — perhaps three days' journey away but as plain as if it were within reach — a final ridge standing between the familiar Indus and the path I want to take. Snow lies on shaded northern slopes of the farthest ridge, sure sign in midsummer

139

that the land must be around 4500 metres. Across this snow I may have to climb if the rope bridge has rotted away, if I have too little food to get back to Lamayuru and if I feel too scared to attempt the riverside rocks to Alchi.

Now, in case the spirit of Prinkiti La can help me on my way, I place a stone on each of the cairns that travellers have built for the spirit of the pass and I start down into the ravine.

Traffic is light. First I meet a lama. He is as fat as an abbot, sits astride a white horse and has a girl of eleven or so walking ahead carrying his walking stick. He stops and asks a question which I suppose means: 'Where are you going?'

'Wonlah,' I reply, which must be the right response because he nods and repeats 'Wonlah' before shaking his reins and getting the horse under way again.

Wonlah is a hill village built on a high knoll above the junction of two streams and all that I know of it, apart from a distant sighting on an earlier walk, I heard from a Ladakhi who works for the Save the Children Fund. He was there showing parents how to mix milk powder. During his demonstration, a farmer on the fringe of the crowd pushed his way forward, elbowed aside the Save the Children Fund worker and began to berate the other Wonlah people. He pointed to the ruins of a castle and demanded to know why no one had any respect for ducal property.

'I am your duke. Yet you steal bricks and stones from the house where my family have always lived. What right have you? I cannot begin to tell you how unhappy it makes me to see you people who ought to know your place just walking up and stealing anything you like from me.

'And that is not all. I own field after field. I know what is my land. And you know what is my land. So how do you explain the way you cultivate my land and take its crops? You cannot explain. You are thieves. Nobody is honest anymore.'

At one point during his harangue the speaker was all authority and calm disdain, the next he collapsed back into a ragged farmer, bent and blinking, silent and looking around as if wondering why everyone was staring agape at him or snickering as if he had been making a fool of himself. Abashed, he slunk back to his place. The others stopped staring and whispering and the Save the Children Fund worker got back to praising the benefits of milk powder.

Afterwards, the fund worker began asking, 'Is that old man really your duke?' People laughed. Of course he wasn't the duke. There hadn't been any dukes around the place for hundreds of years.

'Well, is he a bit, you know, soft in the head?'

Not that they knew. He had never acted like that before. Usually he was quiet and withdrawn.

'And do you steal bits of the castle?'

Why, of course not. Well, you couldn't really call it stealing. They supposed the last duke's family had died out generations and generations ago. So bit by bit, over the years, everyone had started cultivating the duke's land. And if you needed bricks or some dressed stone, it seemed a waste of time to go to any trouble when you could just jemmy a bit of castle apart and use that.

When the Save the Children Fund worker told me of the excitement at Wonlah, he explained it all by saying that the farmer who berated his fellow villagers must have been possessed by the spirit of the duke. I wondered how that could be. Say the spirit of the dead duke had by now been reincarnated through several hundred generations of insects, worms, dogs and what-have-yous, and say he was now a cockroach, would that cockroach know he was once the duke of Wonlah? And would the cockroach also know that the duke's land had been expropriated by the common people and his castle pulled apart? If so, would the cockroach also have the power to fill the shy farmer with the duke's outrage?

But, not being a theologian, I kept silent.

After the lama and I part, I come upon some young women dawdling on their way towards Wonlah. Ladakhi women are supposed to be an outrage to Muslims. Land ownership can pass through females. They can take and dismiss lovers and, instead of marrying one husband, they can marry an entire family of brothers. All the books say so, which may only show that writers find it easier to steal from other books rather than make their own enquiries. I have seen no sign of polyandry. Even so, Ladakhi women are more cheery and open than Muslim women are in public and, on seeing an elderly gent coming carefully downhill, the five women ahead of me — all in their late teens or early twenties — throw themselves into caricaturing the way I walk.

So I toss away caution and switch to a flying goose-step. This they cannot resist. All laughing, we try to race one another downhill with knees locked straight and toes kicking high. I can see what is going to happen. And I do not care. The harder they imitate me, the more their toes tangle in their ground-length gowns. They start to wobble, to cry out and to grasp at each other. Inevitably one loses balance completely, grasps harder at her sisters and brings the lot down in a heap. They seem neither hurt nor chastened. We all laugh. I resume my proper pace and they theirs.

I know I am nearing the end of the ravine when the air fills with attar of roses. The mouth of the gorge is marked by prayer flags strung out like washing on a line, by a colony of chortens and — rising from rocks — a few briar roses whose scent overpowers the air for a hundred metres.

Here the path I am on is met by a track coming down out of another gorge, and along it walks a schoolgirl. She looks about eight; she has in her hand an ancient book of linen cloth stoutly sewn together. And it had to be stoutly sewn to survive. It looks as if it was made during the reign of Edward VII, the fat man who liked to roger all the ladies. Since the book was printed, generations of fingers have spread black smears over its pages, almost obliterating the letterpress.

With a command of the hand the girl stops me, opens her book and chants from it: 'Ox-Pord Uni-Persity is pipty-six mee-liss prom Lon-Don.' I beam and nod and tell her she is very clever. She accepts the praise calmly and hurries ahead, leaving me to fret about how useless education can be. The sentence she read me had only three useable words — is, fifty-six and from. Miles have been replaced by kilometres; Oxford University and London are unimaginably meaningless in this setting. But it's none of my business.

Now the land opens on to a narrow plain. The houses, the monastery and the ruined castle of Wonlah bestride a distant mound; in the foreground lies the deserted hamlet of Shilla — deserted because everybody is out in the fields. A mastiff left guarding a house rushes me. I perform my benign-old-man act, standing still and murmuring soothingly but holding my walking stick at the ready. The dog snarls, twists, barks and shakes its head. Its eyelids are lined with rows of flies that manage to keep their place in spite of the dog's performance.

In time the dog calms and retires to its farmhouse and when I move on a woman and her children hurry towards me across a barley field. I grow puffed up: she must remember me from the time I walked to Shilla two years ago.

Not so. She has merely recognised the stride of a Westerner and is wanting a dose of the pills that Westerners carry with them. She rubs her brow and makes wincing expressions to mime pain. Her children exhibit their scratches.

Before I left home for Choglamsar, my doctor gave me a fair pile of medicines. Most were iron pills because, to acclimatise to altitude, the body produces more red corpuscles, and to do that easily it needs an abundance of iron to draw on. By now I am acclimatised and have iron pills to spare. I think they are harmless, so I give her two and tell her that, if they do not work, it will be because she lacks faith. Understanding nothing, she grins and bobs and gobbles the pills.

And now the children. I bring out a ballpoint and draw circles around each scratch. The children turn silent and round-eyed. Now I produce sticking plaster and apply bits to each marked wound. This is a profoundly impressive procedure. They look as if they want to run off to show their dressings to other children. But they stand still, too awed to move, staring at the places where once they had nothing but naked scratches.

fifteen

Kilometres and kilometres above Shilla, a groyne has been built across the riverbed to divert part of the stream into an irrigation race. Around the hillside the water runs in a skinny canal marked by two hairline streaks of green, one on either bank, where seeping moisture lets plants grow.

By the canal stand a man and his son, who beckon me over. At that point the canal is still about three metres above the floor of the valley and has 500 metres to run before it glides down and enters the main area of Wonlah cropland.

An anthropologist with a handsome study grant might be able to spend a spacious summer discovering why Wonlah irrigation water is not — except for one purpose that I am coming to — allowed on to the land where the man and his son are working. But, for whatever reason, the field where they stand is unwatered. So it grows nothing. Yet they have enclosed it with four stone walls, which they are now capping with ridged mud, into which they are pushing short lengths of thorny twigs. They seem pleased when I admire the way they have secured their barren plot from invasion.

Then the father makes one of those silly-me-what-am-I-thinking-of movements and beckons me to follow. He leads the way to a shoulder-high building that covers about as much ground as an outdoor privy. Here he points to an aged man sitting against the building and twirling a prayer wheel. At the sound of our arrival the old man looks up and stares

144

in our general direction. From his left eye, pus runs steadily down a cheek and into his beard.

In an imperative tone the son addresses me: 'Doc-Torr. Doc-Torr.' Among the stuff my own doctor gave me is a broad-spectrum antibiotic which he said I could use if all else failed. But I do not feel up to gambling with what the tablets might do to the old man. He is, after all, alert, upright and moving easily. So I shake my head. The son accepts my refusal with such easy resignation that I make an enquiring gesture at the little stone hut, and he signals that I may have a look.

It is the family barley mill, and just uphill from it is the one point

Pus runs from the eyes of this Wonlah farmer as he
sits by the family barleymill

145

where water can be drawn from this section of the irrigation canal. A stone has been removed from the bank and a hollow log inserted in its place. Water rushes down the log and strikes the vanes of an undershot grindstone inside the mill. From the ceiling hangs a handwoven woollen sack filled with barley. A tiny hole has been made in one corner of the bag.

On the circumference of the grindstone is a lug through which is threaded a string that runs up to the barley bag. Once on each rotation of the grindstone, the lug tautens the string, which gives the bag a little jiggle that shakes a few grains of barley down on to the unmoving upper millstone. It has a concave face sloping down to a hole, and into this hole fall barley grains. The spinning lower millstone catches and crushes the barley, then centrifugal force tosses barley meal on to the mill floor.

Outsiders sneer at Ladakhis, saying they are so backward that they can think of nothing to do with wheels except to use them to send messages to Heaven. The sneer is only half right. Until China invaded India in 1962, which jolted the Indian army into sending in its road-builders, the old kingdom had no roads, which meant that the near-vertical landscape had no wheeled traffic: donkeys were the sensible way to move stuff around. So the barley mill and its cunning wheels give me a kick. The mill produces a family's staple food at no running cost and is so close to automated that it can be left in the care of children or grandparents.

Now Wonlah is only a stroll away. Midday is coming up and I am still breakfastless after the hooley in the dugout. I climb among the houses looking for a teastall. Good, there is one. Inside squats a young man wearing a green Kashmiri pyjama-suit. He holds a tray of uncooked rice and flicks his fingers through the grains tossing away stones and blowing away dust. He raises a doleful face and looks offended when I ask for tea.

'Is this not the teastall?' I ask.

'Of course. But I am not the teastall man. I am the doctor of Wonlah.'

He is newly graduated and, to repay a government scholarship to university, he has had to leave friends and family, to turn his back on the beauty and civilisation of Kashmir and to work for a pittance and far from a mosque in this forlorn dump where the people are too ignorant to accept his skills, his leadership and his superiority.

The doltish Wonlah farmers, he says, are sunk in disease. He could cure them. But even those who seek his advice spurn him once he has helped them. Always the people are getting gastro-enteritis. Why? Because they drink straight from the stream. At one point he managed to direct the men of Wonlah to dig a pit beside the river. Water seeped into it, crudely filtered but a hundred times safer than direct from the river. Yet what do the stupid and ungrateful people of Wonlah continue to do? They continue — of course — to drink straight from the stream.

I tell him about the old man beside the barley mill whose left eye oozes pus. Yes, yes, he knows all about him. He has given the old man's son medicine for his father but the idiot fails to give it regularly.

'These are stupid and impossible people,' says the doctor of Wonlah. After a silence he adds, 'They are also hypocrites. They keep saying their religion forbids them to catch fish. So them employ me as their fisherman.

'I am their prisoner. I cannot leave. Or the government will make me pay for all my years at university. So they threaten. They are driving me out if I do not catch fish. I, a doctor, must weave nets and catch trouts and perform errands.' His voice rises. 'Lowly errands. Today I run the teastall because this teastall man will visit a lewd woman.'

He turns mocking: 'You will drink tea, sir? Yes, sir. Of course, sir, Elegant scented Kashmiri tea, sir? Rancid Tibetan tea? Sticky Indian char? Yes, sir. Gladly, sir. Please be sitting, sir.'

Thirst makes me rude. 'Indian, thanks.' He scowls. But he makes a pot and for a time he watches me in silence. Then he asks, 'How many sons have you?'

'None. I have two daughters.'

'Where is your wife?'

'I have no wife. She divorced me.'

He looks up with a start. 'How could she divorce you? Women cannot divorce men. Men have to divorce women.'

'It is different in my country.'

'What does your wife live in?'

'A house.'

'But how can a divorced woman have a house?'

'Actually I gave it to her.'

'After she divorced you?'

'Yes.'

This silences him. And the silence stretches out. Then he raises his head, looks straight at me and says, slowly and formally as if reading from a written judgement, 'What you have said proves that our culture is superior to yours.'

To this there is no useful answer, so, without any delicacy, I pay for my tea and am gone.

Hours later, the path I am following enters a narrowing gorge which seems to end in a cliff that looks like an art-deco skyscraper. Radio City, New York, perhaps? The sun, now nearly setting, is at my back. By now it must be overhead at Teheran. The first faint gloom of late afternoon is gathering at the base of the cliff. As I walk, the shadows deepen and start to climb the rocks. I feel the world turning over into night.

Then the path turns hard left. At the bend stands a great house — stabling below, rooms above — in a grove of walnut trees. The family sit among the trees spinning yarn, loading bobbins, weaving cloth. They wave companionably. I turn the bend and climb. Somehow the feeling comes that the bend had a special importance, that it was a boundary and that in crossing it I have entered a world where people do not know the name of their own country because they do not know that beyond the mountains are governments and frontiers and names on maps.

At dusk, the feeling grows. I select a stony bed beside a creek where the water chitters along the base of a cliff of conglomerate rock. This is the plum pudding among rocks, made of boulders lying inside soil that has compressed and turned to stone. I lay out my sleeping bag among truly giant boulders, perhaps two metres tall, and sit there eating.

This brings two women running. They shout at me contemptuously and without any of the slow precision that would show they know it is necessary to articulate carefully when talking to foreigners. When I look stupid and uncomprehending they turn to one another. Their expressions are asking: 'How can a fellow human not understand speech?'

One woman slaps one of the giant boulders and points to the cliff. Understanding comes. She is saying: 'You ignorant little pink man, have you never head of conglomerate rock? Can't you see the size of these boulders that keep falling from the cliff? If you sleep here, you'll get crushed by falling rock. And when that happens, who do you think will be lumbered with the job of scraping you up and giving you a funeral?'

They watch me move my pack and my sleeping bag to safety. Then, duty done, they disappear. It must be the same two women who arrange one more kindness for me. Presently two boys appear, carrying a metal dish loaded with peas in their pods. I eat them for pudding. The boys have hunkered down to watch the strange person eat, and when I get into the sleeping bag and stretch out on the ground, they discuss my actions. It has been a long day since leaving the dugout; the first stars are out; I begin to lose interest in whatever it is that the boys say every time I roll over. Then I wake in sunlight.

sixteen

The land keeps rising. Cultivation has ended. On the slopes no weeds, no grass, no shrubs grow. All is desert and desolation. It is hours since I saw the roofs of the houses from which the boys brought peas. The air grows thinner but I am moving easily. Then, around mid-afternoon, I take a bend and see a sight that makes me want to turn back.

Ahead, the valley ends in a cliff. Up its face curls a zig-zag track that seems to climb forever. Looking at the track, I try to put mental chalkmarks on it to divide it up into hourly bites: a three-hour struggle. And after that, if I am reading the country right, there will be a gentler ascent, then a pass, followed by a jarring descent into the valley that runs down to the Zanskar. Looking at the zig-zag, I can feel my pack fill with bricks and my legs ooze all their strength. Honestly, I can never manage that height. But I move forward, jollied along by pride but keen to kid myself that any sane person would turn back.

From a side valley ahead of me two figures emerge. At the sight of me they stop and wait. If this were a western movie, they would crouch in ambush behind a rock and they would be dirty and unshaven to signal that they rob and kill every stranger they see. Instead, they are dirty because Ladakhis go without baths and handbasins and they are unshaven because they are only fourteen or fifteen.

From beside the track they stare at me. And I stare back. When I am abreast I stop. The boys move to either side of me. Both put out their

150

hands and try to lift my pack from my back. They are using force. But they are not forcible. So I make my arms go slack to let the boys work the shoulder straps free of my body. One of them mimes an offer. He will carry the pack up the zig-zags and then dump it near the snowline where I can pick it up again. I grin and nod. I feel the worry lines on my face melt. I shrug and twist to let the pack fall, then hold it up so the older boy can slide his shoulders into the straps.

Both boys look irrationally pleased, and in haste they are on their way. Why such a hurry, I wonder. Did they fear I might change my mind? Soon they are far above me calling out 'Julay, julay, julay' and moving like driven goats.

I follow, rejoicing at my weightlessness and freedom. Then, in despair, I begin to curse myself. Until late afternoon I must zig and I must zag and at the end of it all I shall see no pack beside the track, no passport, no food, no traveller's cheques, no bottles of water, no sleeping bag, no Rolleiflex. O God, O God, what were you thinking of when you made me so trusting? Why am I so naïve? What have Ladakhis ever done for me that I should completely trust everything I need to those boys?

At the head of the zig-zags, though, my pack stands beside the track, solitary in the solitude of a high pass. Pools of snow lie in the shadow of rocks. The ground continues to rise, but the slope is easy now and the crest is in sight. By the time I reach the pass, I discover I am being followed. A donkey caravan appears, being driven faster than I can walk.

The crest of the pass turns out to be a plateau paved with a sudden collection of scruffy low bushes. When the donkeys come up beside me, the man driving them gives me a sedate greeting. Not so the boy with him. He rushes me, jumping over bushes, throwing up his arms and shouting greetings. This goofing around lasts long enough for me to print his face on my mind and for him to remember me — which he does two days later when I am trying to save a life and am in need of help.

For the moment, though, the donkey-driver growls and calls the boy back to his work. The boy pulls a face, performs a spinning leap and runs back to shout at donkeys and goad them with a stick. The donkey train picks up speed, the track begins to slope downhill and I can feel the day deciding that it must be about time for dusk.

The track begins to level out. Ahead, like stone igloos, huddle nomadic herders' summer huts. And straight ahead of me the track divides into two and passes either side of a deep circular hole that is lined with stone, then capped with a ring of broad flat stones which jut inward to form a solid ledge around the top.

It is a wolf trap. The trick is to dump a clapped-out goat into the hole and walk away. A wolf hears and smells the goat, leaps in and starts eating. When it is done, the overhanging ledge of stones prevents the wolf from hauling itself out. It dies. Its smell attracts another wolf — and so on forever until the world is rid of the last wolf. So much for theory. This trap is clean. Not a bone. Not a skull.

Stopping to admire its workmanship, though, has made me realise I am stonkered. I find a giant flat rock, spread my sleeping bag, chew cheese, nuts, dried apricots and watch nomads lead a line of goats home. They must be late. Darkness is building quickly. But in the dying light one man sees me and waves. When the goats have been led into their fold he turns, climbs to me, sees a plastic cup lying among my packets of food, points to the cup and signals that I am to bring it down with me.

Back at the goat pens, he vaults into a small enclosure in which a solitary nanny stands. Along one edge runs a row of stone boxes with flat stone lids. He removes one lid and, with a vertical leap, a kid emerges and clasps one of the nanny's teats. In silence we watch the little goat drink. Now the man takes a bucket, places it on the floor of the enclosure and holds a hand over the kid's nostrils. When it unclamps itself to gasp for a breath, he lifts it, dumps it in its box and replaces the lid.

Now it is his turn to clasp the teats. Presently under the stars I hear the immemorial sound of milk jets scything through a stiff froth of milk rising in a bucket. The herdsman grabs my cup and pours me a hot nightcap.

On my ledge of flat stone I wake next morning without so much as one wolf bite. But already the pens and the stone igloos are empty. It is too late in the day to wave goodbye to the people in their summer camp. They and other herding families must be on the slopes. But I see no one until I breast a rise and, hours earlier than I had expected, enter a hamlet called Hinju.

From the flat roof of the first house a man leaning against the parapet extends a hand and gives a palm-down beckon. Through ground-floor stabling I walk, climb two flights of twisting stairs and join a family of four on the roof. The bride of the house is in such tatters of homespun that the rotting cloth has fallen away and is revealing her breasts as she spins. The grandfather, also spinning, turns a warrior face and a red-eyed glare at me. And grins. The man who summoned me is seated at a foot-operated loom made of willow branches only just large enough to hold the mortices for its mortice-and-tenon joints: a frail machine to produce the taut dense cloth the man is making. As for the grandmother, she is standing plunging a piston into her gur-gur, the Tibetan churn in which cheesy-tasting butter is forced to amalgamate with hot tea.

As soon as I have finished my cup of tea, the weaver strides to my pack, hauls it over his shoulders and plunges downstairs. Angry, I follow. But he is no runaway robber, only a bellwether using my pack to make me follow him a few kilometres to a lesser hamlet. Hinju Brok it is called and there he opens the door of a one-roomed house.

Inside I follow him to a corner where a pile of dried goatskins is stacked. One by one he tosses them aside. Underneath lies the body of a man.

No I am wrong. It is not a corpse. The eyelids flicker, the eyes focus on the weaver. Tense white lips produce a trembling smile.

The weaver turns down the final goatskin. Around one leg of the sick man is wrapped a rag as filthy as anything I have ever seen. I lift it away. Down the leg lies a vertical gash say ten centimetres long. It runs with pus. The weaver manages to get it across that the man is Tsetan Drorday of Hinju Brok, that nine days ago when he was pollarding willows his axe slipped and gashed his leg — and now it is my duty to save his life.

From the bottom of my pack I pull out all the potions my doctor gave me when I left home: Streptotriad, which is a cure-all antibiotic, mercurochrome antiseptic, iron tablets, a library of sticking plasters and some tablets that are supposed to bung up the bowels.

Beside Tsetan Drorday's door runs a creek in which I dunk one corner of my bath towel before pouring mercurochrome over the dampness. The injured leg is burning to the touch and swollen to twice the size of the other. Gently I work the damp cloth along the bare bone of the wound. Tsetan Drorday whimpers. Next the wound gets drops of raw mercurochrome from top to bottom. From either side of the gash I press the skin together and hold it in place with four narrow strips of sticking plaster.

All the men working in the barley fields of Hinju Brok must have noticed the weaver and me entering Tsetan Drorday's house. They must have dropped their mattocks and shovels and come to look at what is going on because, when I glance up, I see a full gallery of spectators. None of them seems to be objecting to what I am doing. Indeed their interest is straying. In pulling out all my medicine, I have scattered other bits of gear around the mud floor. In this setting, everything I am carrying looks like an indecent flaunting of my opulence.

The men empty my pack and pass everything around for inspection. (Dear God, let them keep their fingers off the Rolleiflex lenses.) I feel another flood of admiration for Ladakhis, because from the corner of an eye, I notice that only one thing produces any excitement or admiration, and that is the one item which would be of sure use to them, a coil of light terylene rope.

To round off what I can do for Tsetan Drorday, I get him to take four Streptotriad tablets, then I drop my towel in the creek, give it a wring out and wrap it around the scalding-hot leg. The clash of cold and hot makes him jump but after that the cooling of the leg must do some good. The tension seeps from his body, he gives me a nod and the pain-tautened lips flicker when he tries another smile.

The day is ending. Tsetan Drorday's fowls stand at his open doorway, hop over the threshold, circle the room and flap up to their roosts on pegs driven into the walls. After they have settled themselves, his wife enters, a small proud-standing woman with a grotesquely large head and a great slab of a face that is missing a few front teeth. A simple perak with a handful of turquoise sewn into it lies over her head, a goatskin hangs down her back, around her neck is suspended a bunch of charms sewn up in leather.

The weaver explains my presence. She inspects the wounded leg and seems to accept my work. I get the impression that tonight I am expected to sleep indoors, sharing the floor with Tsetan Drorday and his wife.

But first she must prepare dinner. At this rainless height of bare rock, wood is too precious to burn and, anyway, willow — which is the only tree that manages to survive alongside streams — is poor, sparky firing. So the dried dung of yaks and dzos, which are a cattle-yak cross, is used on chimneyless hearths. It is a slow and sullen fuel, but dung does hold a glimmer all day and, squatting by her fireplace, Tsetan Drorday's wife scratches among dung ash, finds an ember and presses a scrap of tinder against it. The tinder seems to be the dried root of a little shrub, a euphorbia of some sort, that old people are sent in autumn to harvest from hillsides and to bring down by the donkeyload.

Patiently, she blows and blows and blows at it. The tinder flares. With a spare hand she crumbles dung over it. The dung catches. She withdraws the euphorbia root, rubs out the flame on it and puts it aside for next time. On to the dung fire goes a pot to make tea. Without flicking the dung crumbs from her hand, she scoops up a handful of roasted barley meal and dumps it into a bowl. The only utensil in the house that does not look homemade is an empty Carlsberg lager can with no top. From it she dribbles water into the barley meal and starts to knead it with dungy fingers.

I bring out my own meal: walnuts, dried apricots and a lump of vile processed cheese. In Leh, where I bought it all, it seemed poor stuff; here it looks an extravagance.

When the woman has made a paste of barley meal, she eats some of it herself — this is tsampa, the universal food of the Himalayas — and then adds more water to make a gruel. She takes the bowl to Tsetan Drorday and tries to lift him up, but his cries say the pain is too great. So she cradles his head and helps him to drink from the bowl.

By now I am in my sleeping bag, but before Tsetan Drorday's wife can sleep she has prayers to say. From the waist up she bares herself, falls to her knees and throws her torso forward, leans on her forearms and rests her brow in the dust. Three times she repeats these prostrations before rising and coming over to me. I am lying with my head to the west, and this seems to offend her. (Did Marie Stopes not believe that things go wrong unless you are pointing the right way when asleep?) So, under the direction of the woman, I jiggle around to lie east-west. She nods in satisfaction and disappears under goatskins.

At some stage during the night, Tsetan Drorday groans in such pain that I wake. And I wonder what to do. I become convinced that he has gangrene. I remember a government dispensary at Saspul, over the mountains and beside the Indus. Tomorrow, I decide, I shall find a foot track, which my map says runs uphill around here, and crosses those sheets of snow that I saw from Prinkiti La. The track then descends to Alchi. From there I can cross the new bridge over the Indus and walk upstream to Saspul. There I shall get the doctor at the dispensary to cross the mountains to Hinju Brok and cut off Tsetan Drorday's leg.

How clear and plain night thoughts can be, how easily they cut through difficulty. Getting to Saspul must take three days at least. Of course the doctor at the dispensary will be able to spare six days' walking. Naturally he has knives and saws ready for roadside amputations. When he gets here he will have no trouble showing a sensible farmer — or the weaver of Hinju, — how to hold a chloroform pad over Tsetan Drorday's nostrils.

Content with my decision, I sleep again. At sunrise the plan is still holding firm.

Tsetan Drorday's wife emerges from her animal skins, I from my hi-tech sleeping bag. She eats the remains of last night's tsampa gruel. Again I eat nuts, apricots and cheese. I dose Tsetan Drorday with more Streptotriad, pour raw mercurochrome over the closed line of his wound, douse the towel in the creek and rewind it around his leg in the hope the wet chill may ease pain. To his wife I give the remainder of the antibiotics and act out a set of instructions: he must have two tablets thrice daily after meals.

I hear what I think is Tibetan for 'I bring doctor' emerge from my lips and see no sign of understanding on her face: either I have got it wrong or the Ladakhi used here has strayed too far from its source. Or she has never heard of doctors.

Then I hoist my pack and am gone, puffed up with a fresh attack of *Boys' Own Annual* heroism. Again I am that fine young Carstairs fellow, steady eyes lifted to the peaks that I must cross, clean-cut jaw jutting, muscles rippling all over the place, my lofty mind filled with the white man's duty.

It turned out to be an attack I could have done without.

By early afternoon I had veered off from the main valley and, following the map, was crossing a scree slope on a track that was leading to a village called Sumdah, which seemed to be around 4000 metres. After that it would be a plod to a pass at 5000 metres — a plod which I was beginning to realise I would never make.

The spirit of Carstairs had let me down. Instead of the morning's quick, confident, swinging strides I ought to have governed my speed and rationed the energy being spent on the valley floor so that there might have been some left over for the afternoon's climb. Instead, when I needed spare power to call on, my legs were feeling like sodden paper and no amount of resting could get my breath back. Into Sumdah I stumbled, certain of failure. I stood leaning brokenly on my walking stick.

For a time Sumdah seemed to be empty of people. Then a figure approached. And our faces lit. He was the donkey boy who, two days before, had pranced around me when we were crossing the scrubby plateau. We had no words in common and when I asked, 'Is there anyone here who would act as porter for me?' he walked away, but with a sign that I must follow. He led me to a low building on the outskirts of the village. Together we entered and found ourselves in a familiar setting: rows of cramped desks, silent children staring and a teacher turning from his blackboard.

I gabbled about a man dying at Hinju Brok, about having to get to the dispensary at Saspul. With one question the teacher silenced me: 'Do you enjoy intoxication?' When I nodded, he dismissed his class for the day and led me into a bedroom lying off his classroom. He lifted a brass ewer and poured two cups of chang.

He was called Nawang Geler, meaning Nawang the teacher; he was in his twenties and he told me that he had travelled as far east as Assam and as far south as Madras, a wide range for a Ladakhi because Ladakhis are among the poorest people in India. Like the doleful doctor of Wonlah, Nawang Geler was freshly graduated and was now paying for his education by taking on work in this remoteness. Unlike the doctor, though, he belonged to his surroundings and over the following days I was to enjoy watching the way he could fit in with everybody we met, dropping into conversation with strangers as if, after some brief pause, they were simply resuming an old discussion.

But this was for the future. As we sat drinking chang, he managed to calm me and to understand about Tsetan Drorday, his need for the doctor at Saspul and my inability to carry on with a loaded pack on my back. 'So I need someone to carry my pack. I'll pay a porter a hundred rupees to come with me.'

A hundred rupees. That was about a week's wages for a teacher. Nawang Geler announced, 'I am your porter.' He asked if he could carry his own gear in my pack. I said 'Of course', and he showed me what he

Monk in his cell at Wuleh Tokpo.

wished to carry: a muslin bag full of damp grains, a metal jug and another bag of barley meal for tsampa. In among my elaborate supply of stuff went his provisions. We rose, he strapped on my pack and we were on the road.

For him it seemed an easy stroll. For me, it was a disagreeable and bad-tempered climb. Why did he move so easily? Why did he not stop and puff whenever I needed a breather? Why did he get 500 metres ahead of me and then stand, a picture of such suffering patience that I felt forced to hurry? And then, as soon as I caught up with him and stood gasping, why did he instantly rush on ahead? And why, when the most extraordinary sight opened up in front of us, did he not appreciate my suffering when I fell to the ground at the base of a chorten unable to move any more?

By then we must have reached the 4500-metre line. Since leaving Sumdah we had seen no sign, apart from the track itself, that other people ever rose this high, and I had imagined that not until we reached Alchi on the following night would we see any buildings larger than some herding family's summer shelter. Instead, when I stumbled, fell and would not move, we were at the walls of two structures so large that, even in a city, they might have looked notable. One seemed to be a village built as a single apartment house so that, in winter, the inhabitants could visit one another under cover.

The other building — five storeys high? six even? — was a monastery. The story behind it was that some mythical monastery-builder far away in another part of the Zanskar catchment still had some paint left over after decorating the walls of another monastery he had just completed. So, to use up his leftover paint, he lifted himself into the air and, carrying his paint and brushes, flew here to start work on yet another monastery.

For a good five minutes, though, I could not give a toss what magical builder had placed the monastery here nor even whether I should live. While I lay collapsed Nawang Geler threw his head back, cupped his hands and shouted salvoes of 'Julay, julay, julay' at the rooftop of the monastery. Aloft, a figure leaned over a parapet and yelled back. By the time I was showing any interest, a monk had come down to his front door and Nawang Geler was trying to jolly me into getting on my feet and tottering over to the monastery.

Once inside, it was only a matter of twisting up five or six flights of stone stairs, using the wall to help me support myself. Reaching the flat roof, where we were to spend the night, must have perked me up because soon I was spry again and was going around behind the solitary lama who lived in this palace of a monastery.

The floors below may have been jammed with chrysoprase, chalcedony and pearls. I don't know. The lama didn't show me. The treasures on the rooftop were enough to have me gasping, not that they were magnificent in their own right, only that it was inconceivable that they could even have reached this height, this isolation, this lonely emptiness.

In one worship room a pierced screen carved in the round stretched from wall to wall, portraying the beasts and demons of the Tibetan hell. It must have been seven metres long and two high. It would have taken unimaginable labour to bring it here — and an even greater and more delicate struggle to shield it from people's hands, because between the screen and the space where people worshipped stood a sheet of glass that completely isolated the carving.

It could scarcely have come from the valley I was trying to climb out of. The only way it could have arrived was in the hands of a team of men who must have eased the glass off the tray of a truck where the road ends at Alchi. Then, carefully holding it, they must have climbed to 5000 metres, crossed the pass and descended a narrow track to the monastery and then climbed the twisting staircase, while growing increasingly alarmed that, in the final minutes, the sheet of glass might tap against a wall and shatter.

In two other worship rooms stood identical Buddha figures, not large but something over life-size. Because one room stood just off the lama's kitchen, one sculpture was blackened from cooking fires. The other was still pure white and undecorated. The flying monastery-builder must finally have run out of paint.

Apart from the kitchen and worship rooms, the roof was bare. On three sides, high walls gave wind protection. Inside the walls ran three colonnades holding up a narrow horseshoe roof. Within this peristyle the lama, Nawang Geler and I slept on the floor, except for a wakeful pause when I peed over a low parapet on the fourth wall. By then I had recovered from the climb. The moon was a few days off full; the rest of the sky was paved from horizon to horizon with a fluorescent sheet of stars without a gap of black between them. All around me, like some frozen storm at sea, stretched whitecap mountains: motionless waves whose edges glowed from the billions of lights above.

Morning comes. Nawang Geler and I climb through absolute desolation. Back at the monastery, a few briars grew from cracks in the rocks. Now everything is bare. With every step we enter a worse world. More and more mountaintops appear. Grey, black, brown rocks stretch to infinity, and still we have not reached the snow sheets I saw four days ago. I have emptied my water bottles. And still my mouth is dry and foul-tasting. My lips are rimmed with white slime. I brush it away. It reappears.

Self-pity grows. And again I rage inside in another I-hate-Nawang-Geler mood. Here I am, a little old man who could be his grandfather, pushing myself uphill on my walking stick. And what does he do for me? Nothing. He just skips ahead leaving me to struggle and moan. Look at him now, the swine. He has been galloping ahead along a great curve in the track. He is a kilometre ahead, lolling at his ease. He seems to have dropped my pack beside a rock that juts from a scree slope. By God,

Bringing home the firewood.

162

when I get up there I'll give him a piece of my mind, you see if I don't.

But when, trembling, I do get there, I turn wobbly with gratitude. At the base of a great rock a spring drips water. Nawang Geler has collected it in his metal jug. And into the jug he has dipped and squeezed that bag of damp grains that he packed. It is barley that has been put through the chang-making process. When I arrive, he gives the bag one final squeeze and offers me the jug to drink from. My mouth fills with the thirst-killing acidity of chang. I give him a grin. He takes his swig. We climb companionably.

Suddenly we are in snow. Then we are standing looking over the far edge of the hills. Five thousand metres! Alone I have made it. By uncomplaining struggle, I have turned myself into one of the world's immortal heroes. I prepare to clamp a fist over my heart and raise the other hand in triumph as if posing for a statue of myself. But at my feet I see a heap of donkey dung to remind me that this is no feat of mountaineering. We have only spent the morning walking along the Sumdah-Alchi highway: an easy stroll for a Ladakhi five-year-old.

All afternoon we head downhill. When it is nearly time for pre-dinner drinks in the apricot-dotted courtyard of the little mud-brick hotel at Alchi, we are emerging from a gorge. The ground has grown level. The barley fields are in view. The hotel is just around the corner.

Where irrigation water spills and makes a tiny waterfall a European woman and a man are standing splashing their faces. Looking up, she sees Nawang Geler and me approaching, me in front, he carrying my pack. In English she whispers to her husband, 'Look, dear, here is a traveller with his servant.' Passing them, I bow and slightly raise my walking stick in salute. And I feel like brave little Tintin.

seventeen

Next morning, early and urgent, I head off for the doctor at Saspul. The land is easy and level, except for a rock where the track enters a narrow defile, rises and falls. From the crest I see a man approaching. On his side of the pathway up the rock there is barely room for two. So I wait and lean aside to let him pass.

He says, 'G'day.'

I say, 'G'day.'

He looks at my boots and must recognise their make because he says, 'Shit, you're a bloody New Zealander.'

'Yup.'

He grows tense, says he is a New Zealander too, and snaps, 'You gotta tell me. Is Muldoon still in power?'

When I tell the man Muldoon is still prime minister it is as if I have been torturing him with whip and spear. He slumps, looks desperate, then rallies and seems to be getting ready to attack me. Instead blasphemies cascade from his mouth. Then he explains all. When Muldoon became prime minister the man took off for Ethiopia and vowed never to return home until Muldoon had been deposed. In Ethiopia he discovered what a great disadvantage the rest of the world is forced to live under: they never hear a whisper of news from New Zealand.

The years passed. The exiled man began to develop a taste for high barren country. When Ethiopia grew stale, he slipped into Iran, crossed into Afghanistan, roamed the North-West Frontier Province of Pakistan. He could not help noticing that the trend of his travels was getting him ever closer to home and he began to sense that he was about ready to return. In the end he convinced himself: 'Surely to Christ, they've kicked the bastard out by now.' In Delhi he booked himself a flight home. Now he has only a couple of weeks left. He will leave Ladakh, get down to Bombay, hop in a plane and, overnight, will be home again — back under the jackboot of the Muldoon regime.

I want to sit down and comfort the man. Instead I explain why I am in a rush, and leave him to suffer on his own.

At the Saspul dispensary they are having a quiet day. Two men are sitting on the front verandah, their chairs tipped back, their feet resting on the verandah rail. Between them stands a table on which rests a bowl of small apricots. The younger man wears a black Stetson pulled down over his eyes, a chequered shirt, jeans and cowboy boots. He spits out an apricot stone and actually says, 'Howdy, stranger.'

He is the doctor. I start a panicky gabble: Over the hills. Dying man. Got gangrene. Needs leg amputated. Urgent. Let's get moving, huh?

'Let's just take things calmly, fella.'

He whistles for the nurse to bring me a chair, introduces me to his friend, who is the director of the state apricot-breeding station next door, and sends the nurse to pick me a dish of apricots.

'I was raised in Basgo, down the road a piece,' he says. 'Round these parts you gotta realise one thing. Folks livin' behind them thar hills . . .'

I stare at him in disbelief. When he was at medical school did he spend his entire time watching westerns? Or is he just back from a scholarship at a university at one of the south-western states?

'. . . folks livin' behind them thar hills, they're too goddamn backward to take to modern medicines. It's a plain waste of time doctorin' to 'em.'

I must be looking furious with him. He raises a calming hand and says, 'Okay, describe this fella's house to me.'

I tell him. Mud floors. Chickens roosting inside. Chimneyless fire. Dried

165

goatskins stacked in corners. The foul cloth that I removed from Tsetan Drorday's wound.

'You ain't exactly describin' an operatin' theatre to me, are you? Look, say I could rustle up an anaesthetist. Say we both had a spare six days to walk there and back. And say we operated. What's gonna happen? You know what's gonna happen. Before we can slap a bandage on the stump it's gonna be crawlin' six deep with germs. He'll be dead in days. Amputate or do nothing. The result's the same. He's dead meat.'

My face must be curled in contempt because he takes another tack. 'Just run through them symptoms for me again, will ya?'

I try again. Slashed leg. Pus everywhere. Flesh blown up to double its normal size. Shin burning to the touch. Red inflammation.

'That ain't gangrene you're describin', fella. Gangrene goes cold, skin turns all brown. An' you gave him a whole handful of antibiotics, huh?'

I nod.

'Well, say we got the President's very own doctor up from Delhi an' put him in there with a chopper, that's what he woulda done, too. Maybe you overdosed him and made him worse, maybe you hit it about right. Ain't nothin' more anyone else can do.'

He whistles again. The nurse comes. He orders tea for me. While we wait he comes to a sudden decision, stands and orders me to follow. The heels of his cowboy boots click on the wooden floor. He kicks open a door. We stand in the heart of the government dispensary. Shelves line the walls. On them stand empty bottles labelled with the names of all the supplies he needs but cannot get. He has aspirins. He has iodine. He has a dozen other bottles with stuff in them. 'See?' he asks.

'I think I see.'

'Ain't easy,' he says.

On the verandah we drink tea. We shake hands. I thank him for listening.

'Any time, fella.' The words fall, weighted with weariness and lack of hope.

166

I start the walk back to Alchi. Oven-hot gusts are rushing down the valley. I trudge, noticing nothing but the stench coming off my own clothes and body. Through winter, spring and half of summer I have neither bathed nor showered. At Hinju Brok my clothes became saturated with the smells of Tsetan Drorday's house: stale smoke plus something like regurgitated cheese.

Back at Alchi I get soap from my pack and head for the river. Here the Indus powers down the gorge. Only a fool would enter. I search for a backwater, any patch of calm. A tributary is waterfalling down the walls of the gorge, rushing over rocks and being absorbed into the stillness of a mud-paved pond. On a rock I soap, pound and squeeze my clothes, rinse them and spread them on rocks too hot to touch. From my body and out of my hair I wash accumulated smells. My towel is at Hinju Brok. But in the gorge the wind is as hot as if it were coming from a hairdrier, and on the rocks my clothes need only one more turning before they are dry.

Waiting to dress, I hunker down beside the pond. A current is moving the suds away. Already the mud I stirred up is settling. Across the mud moves a watersnail, leaving behind itself a frilled furrow to show where it has passed.

The snail brings General Cunningham to mind. Last century he wrote a thick black-bound book telling everything there was to know about Ladakh, and over the years of reading and rereading him I have allowed the suspicion to enter my mind that Cunningham may have been a bit of a know-all. In all of Ladakh, he wrote, there are no molluscs at all.

So I am glad to see the watersnail and its wrinkled track. I send it a smile. But something happens when the ends of my lips move up. They freeze. Then they twist down. And down my sun-dried face I feel tears moving.

I had better rush. The autumn term starts tomorrow. So straight after breakfast I do a quick farewell tour of the Alchi temples, then strike out for Saspul.

I don't know whether to say goodbye to the doctor. After yesterday's hint that he knows his job is pointless would he feel embarrassed to see me again? I don't risk it. Instead I sit at a table on a platform between the Saspul teastall and the road and wait for a bus or a truck I can hitch a ride on.

An army convoy approaches. All the trucks but one roll by. The truck that does not pass pulls up beside the teastall. I stare at the driver. He refuses to notice.

Out on to the platform steps the teastall man, who starts behaving as if he were an actor in a silent movie. He raises his right arm, holds the

Temples at Alchi, and snow that the Saspul doctor
would not cross.

168

hand, palm down, to his brow. He scans the road, looking left towards Leh and right toward Khalse. Now he looks at the truck driver, who picks up the signal: All clear.

Both men nod. The driver gets out of the cab and walks to the tray of the truck. Now the teastall man joins him and repeats his road-scanning performance. He gives more nods to the driver to assure him that all is safe, that no one is watching. The driver unties a corner of the tarpaulin that covers his cargo. Both men unite in another run-through of the goofy lookout routine.

All is still clear. The driver lifts a bit of tarpaulin. The teastall man slips his hand inside, withdraws a bottle of rum, presses it against his waist, bends double to shield it from view. Still doubled over, he scurries into the teastall.

Now he re-emerges, upright, head held back, eyes casually roaming the sky to indicate carefree innocence.

At the rear of the truck, driver and teastall man click back into lookout pose. Again the driver lifts the tarpaulin. The teastall man extracts another bottle, bends over, runs inside, strolls back.

But this time there really are people watching. From downriver two soldiers are coming up the middle of the road in loopy scissor-leap dancesteps. With every leap they throw their arms out. They stand still. Bow to one another. They flash smiles. They sing. They are in some sort of ecstasy. But it cannot be from drink: they are too steady on their feet.

The teastall man and the driver study the dancing soldiers. They give a shrug to announce that the soldiers are harmless and return to the elaborate caution that advertises their thieving. The dancing soldiers pass the truck and join me on the platform. When the owner offers them tea they wave him away, pull out filter-tipped Panama cigarettes, roll them between their palms, then squeeze and tap until the tobacco falls out into a cupped palm. Each man takes a pinch of brown powder from a tin and sprinkles it over the tobacco. Scowling at the effort, they dribble their enriched tobacco back into the paper tubes, tamp down the tobacco, light up and let out ecstatic sighs. Cigarettes finished, they leap from the teastall platform, run diagonally over the road, perform an elaborate swinging turn and resume their scissor-leaps along the road.

Behind the truck, the others perform their final rum-run. When the driver is back behind the wheel, I give a swing of the thumb to beg a lift. He stares me in the eye, turns down the ends of his mouth, closes his eyes and shakes his head.

Not to worry. Soon the Khalse-Leh bus arrives. Already it is nearly full, and on board it is offering two entertainments. Passengers can let their eyes graze over a young Ladakhi woman with a face of wonderful freshness or they may prefer to study a dead soldier lying in the aisle.

The woman is wearing something I have never seen before, a spanking brand-new perak. Sniffily I think the fore-and-aft top-piece is carrying too much cheap filling of baroque freshwater pearls. She would look more important with more turquoise, more coral. Over the years I suppose she will add to the wealth on her head. Meantime she looks young and fresh and merry. And beside her she is showing off another new possession: one husband.

Straight after Saspul the road swings left away from the river and starts climbing into a series of wrenching bends. Passengers haul fragrant twigs from the pouches of their gowns, pluck leaves, roll them tight and stuff them up their nostrils. That done, a few settle down, knowing the leaves will prevent carsickness. The less confident pull old cans from deeper recesses and hold them near their chins, ready.

The bride in the new perak does neither. But she starts to gasp and to shuffle around on her bottom. Above her upper lip sweat gathers. With her right hand she clutches at her new gown where it is tight against the neck and pulls it away from her. Like a calf that will not be driven to the slaughterboard she looks about with quick and desperate movements. She elbows her husband. He stands and pulls down the upper half of the window. She jolts him aside and tries to thrust her head out. But the size of her spreading perak imprisions her. Vomit dribbles on to her clothes.

170

She sits and stares ahead in horror.

Every few kilometres tracks lead from invisible villages down to the roadside where passengers wait. All seats are now full. More people cannot board unless they are willing to stand on the soldier's corpse. The driver climbs from his seat and kicks the soldier, who raises his trunk into the sitting position, opens his eyelids and, with eyeballs that seem to be still asleep, works out that he is being required to make room. No trouble. He crosses his legs and, as bendy as a snake, tips forward, rests his head on his knees and goes back to sleep.

Dusk is spreading when we reach Leh. I visit every restaurant in town hoping to find a familiar face. But the town is full of strangers. One, a woman, is alone at a table and says she does not mind if we share the space. She is an American, has been in Ladakh two days and says she is getting things sussed out. When did I arrive, she asks. 'Twenty minutes ago.'

This is a satisfactory answer. She is able to tell me she has identified the palace and where to get the best view of it. She recommends the best shop for souvenirs, tells me how to find the bus station and lists day trips people can make. I am glad of her company. Tonight is full moon but it will not be moonrise till later. So, if it were not for her conversation, I might have rushed my meal and been tempted to start walking home in the dark.

The food I am eating is a sort of chow mein that leaves behind a delicious sauce which chopsticks cannot manage. So when the fluent American is briefly silent and a waitress in Tibetan clothes is passing I call, 'Nga-la tooma chick, nung-ro' — to me spoon one, please.

In a fury the waitress abuses me in English: 'How dare you speak to me like that? Don't you know that 'tooma' is a word you only use to servants? Servant! I *own* this place.'

It all eats time. And it does not delay moonrise.

When there is enough light I am on the road, and the road is busy with men who seem not to want to be noticed. Everybody has a bundle and

171

averted eyes — everyone except for three men well spaced out and apparently travelling individually. All are walking bent forward with ropes over their shoulders hauling logs along the middle of the road. We meet and we pass in silence. The full moon has its own etiquette.

When I am abreast of the Indo-Tibetan Border Police barracks, the dog pack that lives there rushes and barks. But the dogs keep their distance. Their threats, though, make me edgy when I reach Choglamsar. We have not one pack but two. They are rivals. They know their own territory. One of the packs knows my smell. I am one of theirs. I cannot pretend to be under their protection. But at least I am under their sufferance. I do not have to fear them. The other pack, though? Whichever way I go I must cross its private gangland and I'm not too sure that I can do it safely.

Past the old people's home I go, past the houses of the permanent staff, across a bit of open ground, through a hole in a wall and out on to the football ground. Safe! At last there is no shelter for the pack to wait in ambush. Not a growl have I heard, not a bark nor the racing thud of the pack's paws. I am almost within reach of the stone wall on the far side of the football ground. This is the boundary. In less than fifteen seconds I shall step across the frontier and be in home territory.

I am congratulating myself but still clutching my walking stick firmly when a silent cloud of dogs rises from the football field and throws me to the ground. Six dogs? Ten dogs? A mass of them, anyway, all scratching, tearing, snarling, biting. I can see where stones that I fell on have ripped my arms. I see blood running. I also see my walking stick rise up and I feel my hand judder when the stick lands with terrible force across the spine of the pack leader. He howls in pain and runs. The others follow.

Up on to my walking stick I haul myself. Bright in the moonlight, say only thirty paces away, I see my door. When I am sitting on my bed it is a toss-up whether my hands are too shaky to handle disinfectant and sticking plaster or are so trembly that they cannot be trusted to pour a glass of rum. I think about disinfectant. But instead I give the hands a tryout with the rum bottle. They seem to manage quite adequately.

eighteen

My wild and romantic excursion is over. When next the sun touches the refugee camp it feels as if no time has passed, nothing has happened.

All the children from Jhun Thang are back from their families' yak-hair tents, looking as if they have never been away on holiday.

Dawa Metok has walked up the valley from her home in the rubbish dump outside the palace walls. Sonam Dakpa has crossed the road from Choglamsar village and is ready to spend another term monitoring my performance to make sure I am teaching the others properly. When I reach the quad to listen to morning chants he shifts his head, faces me and bestows a look of approving recognition. What have I done to earn this honour?

Chanting ends. Now the autumn term can begin. It will bring weeks of pain and jumpiness. The school will destroy Sonam Dakpa. He will disappear as if he had never existed. The discipline master will inflict vile punishment on Dawa Metok. Afterwards she will lie in a long coma. I shall fly home not knowing whether she survives.

But before any of this can happen the school must endure a Sargasso season of that same enforced, despairing indolence that sailors know when winds die, water turns oily, sails sag and dull silence is cracked only by blocks and rigging slapping as the unseen heave of the sea sends masts and booms rolling.

During these first few weeks of the term, dead days accumulate when teachers disappear on pet projects and take pupils away without notice. Dorjee Gyaltsen has rounded up the best dancers and taken two busloads down to Srinagar to give concerts around the city. And whenever he chooses, the sportsmaster plucks athletes out of classes and gives them special training for sports day.

Resentful but as meek as ewes, we other teachers mutter. How are we ever to catch up with lessons if pupils are constantly being seduced from classrooms? Does no one realise that summer will soon slip into autumn and with cold days will come all the fretfulness and urgency of exams that will decide our pupils' lives? If the seniors fail they will be sentenced to a choiceless existence up on the icy plateau of Jhun Thang. Not that the alternative looks marvellous. The children who pass will be shoved another year nearer teachers' training college, another year nearer the chance to step on to the bottom rung of a shabby middle-class career in front of a blackboard, another year nearer becoming the pride and grief of their parents: pride in their success, grief when, like all second-generation immigrants, they abandon their parents' ways, wear jeans and Walkmans and use cigarettes instead of snuff.

Some time after these becalmed weeks I slowly begin to notice that Sonam Dakpa has become trapped in some invisible trouble. He sits at his desk, textbook, exercise book and pen in front of him. And he does nothing. When I am explaining the day's lessons he focuses on an invisible mark on the wall behind my back. His body looks passive. The light in his eyes has gone out. The tension that used to invade his back and shoulders when his brain was racing mine has now melted into apathy.

When the other children do the problems that I have put on the blackboard, his hands lie on his desk. His eyes still engage the wall. If I show impatience with his behaviour he tries not to let my staring or my scowls worry him. But after a time my attention grows too much. He lets loose a put-upon sigh, then he picks up his pen and moves it on the pages of his exercise book. At the end of lessons the books are collected so that, after dinner, I can mark the children's work. And every night when I reach

Sonam Dakpa's book I find page after page empty except for tense little doodles, one to a page.

In the world I come from, his behaviour would create a stir. Teachers would meet to talk about how they could steer him past his troubles. His class teacher might cross the road, go into Choglamsar village and find his widowed mother's house and see if she knew what had killed his interest in schoolwork. All the staff would put out their antennae for rumours. Is his mother so poor that the two of them are having to starve themselves? Is there another child, a sister so sick that she is dying in front of the family's eyes? Has the mother taken a lover whom Sonam Dakpa hates?

In the setting I know, the school counsellor would employ a practised charm to make this troubled pupil unbutton his mind and share his worries. The teachers who had formed themselves into the Sonam Dakpa committee would be torn by a high-minded dispute over whether to photocopy his doodles and send them off to the school psychology service. Half the teachers would object to such a sneaky invasion of privacy. Older hands would lose patience: 'Christ, he'll never bloody *know*. If it helps, do it.'

But here nothing happens. School rule No. 17 states that parents may not question staff decisions. The other, unstated, side of that rule is that if there is trouble at home the few parents who live nearby know that nobody wants them to drop in and talk it over with the teachers.

I, too, do nothing. Some days I stare at Sonam Dakpa and wish I were a sergeant-major turning purple with rage and shouting, 'Dumb insolence gets nowhere with me, young man. I've broken better boys than you.' Other days I tell myself there is no need to do anything, that I have more patience than Sonam Dakpa, that everything will settle down and go back to normal. All I have to do is keep my temper and everything will blow over.

But it turns out that he has more patience than I can muster. Two weeks into his silence, my own fretfulness gets me down. I decide we must talk, I must try to bring his spirits back. At the end of the morning session I dismiss the class and say, 'Sonam Dakpa, you are to stay behind.'

The others stand and stream out. Sonam Dakpa also stands and joins the flow. I move over and stand in front of him. He steps sideways and tries to pass. I grab his shoulder. It is a shock to touch him. Between his bones and my palm I feel no flesh, only a skeleton as slight as a bird's.

My grabbing him alerts the class. They stop and turn. I suppose they expect a thrashing and do not want to miss it. The discipline master's attacks on children have become the school's most common entertainment and by now the kids must be addicted to watching thrashings. Keeping a grip on Sonam Dakpa's shoulder, I shoo the others out of the room and shut the door. The others scuttle sideways to the window. Their faces peer in. Instantly I know my plan has become a wreck. Getting Sonam Dakpa to emerge from his mind's hiding place was probably doomed anyway. But now the sheet of faces across the window, all watching and wanting the excitement of violence, is pushing him further into the recesses of his mind.

I begin my spiel. But my mouth can taste its pointlessness. 'Sonam Dakpa, what's got into you? You've got the best brains in the class. If you keep at it, you could make anything of your life. Why not start work again? It's more fun than just staring at the wall.'

He has already stopped staring at the invisible mark on the wall. He has turned his face to gaze into mine. And he is not finding it very interesting. He does not even bother to give a shrug to signal to me what a boring little man I am. He merely stares as if I am some sort of insect that once seemed interesting but has now turned out to be common and unimportant.

'Okay, Sonam Dakpa, you can go now.'

In no hurry, he walks out into the quad.

Three days later, Sonam Dakpa's life at the school comes to an end. I am not there to see but I hear the story from Dorjee Gyaltsen and, in a sudden burst of speech, from Kelsang Gyatso, the teacher-torturer who took me on that silent chang-drinking picnic beside the river.

Independently they tell me that they saw the discipline master attack Sonam Dakpa in the quad. It was not one of the discipline master's set-piece thrashings up on the concrete block in the quad but an impromptu assault. The man was armed with a length of framing timber — say three metres long and a hundred millimetres by fifty — and was trying to strike Sonam Dakpa on the skull. The boy had backed up against a wall, which probably saved his life, because the more infuriated the discipline master grew, the more wild became his aim and a good half of the blows struck the mud-brick wall. For the rest, Sonam Dakpa either ducked or fended off with a forearm.

Other teachers rushed in. Kelsang Gyatso and Dorjee Gyaltsen said they were frightened that, if no one halted the attack, Sonam Dakpa could easily have been killed. But there was no need to restrain the discipline master. The fatigue of wielding the framing timber caught up with him. He paused a moment to get breath, and there he stood, slumped a little and gasping. In that stillness Sonam Dakpa used the weight of his slight body to land a punch right on the discipline master's nose.

Immediately the teachers closing in to rescue Sonam Dakpa from death were so shocked by his breach of school discipline that they turned on the boy, grabbed him and hauled him off to the headmaster's office. He was instantly expelled.

Sonam Dakpa's punch caused days of indignation among the teachers. In their minds, punching a teacher was such a threat to the good government of the school that his name could barely be spoken. Some turned from me when I asked what would now happen to him. Dorjee Gyaltsen told me that Sonam Dakpa's mother had called on the director and, in defiance of rule No. 17, questioned her son's expulsion and asked for him to be taken back. No. Impossible, said the director.

So she crossed the road, called on the abbot of Choglamsar monastery and persuaded him to let Sonam Dakpa join the monastery school. It is only a tiny school of fifty or so boys who are either drifting into the priesthood or getting a secular education. So every time I go over to the monastery to change my library book I keep a lookout for Sonam Dakpa. I am not sure why, but I suppose I hope that a smile and a question about how things are going may make the world an easier place for him.

Never once, though, do I see him again.

nineteen

The buses here have an iron ladder at the rear that runs up to a roof rack. On long trips, the rack is filled with luggage; on local trips, the ladder and the rack are useful for a free ride. As the bus pulls away, the quick, the nimble and the penniless race after it, leap on to the ladder, climb up and sit in the rack. I did it once myself. The rack is more comfortable than being jam-packed inside, the air is better, the view unimpeded and the whole experience is elevated by the thrill of naughtiness.

When Dorjee Gyaltsen and his troupe of dancers return from Srinagar, the luggage on the rack is crowned with a clutch of inexplicable parcels, each neatly wrapped in strips of thick brown paper, heavily greased to keep rust from the contents.

The evening after his return he comes over to me at rum time, carefully clutching the parcels. One is round, one triangular and the other free-form. He places them on my floor, shakes my hand, says 'Ronner-la' and beams. He seems to be in a state of intense pride and excitement but he keeps the cause of it to himself until he has had his first sip and has exhaled a great and grateful 'Ah'.

Then he makes his announcement: 'I have bought a bicycle.'

With these words the parcels explain themselves: a triangular frame, wheels in the round parcel, handlebar, seat, chain, tool kit and mudguards in the free-form package. A new bike in Ladakh! This will create a sensation. The first time I ever came to Ladakh, the army had trucks, and

179

twice a week Srinagar buses arrived and left. The only other vehicle was an iron-wheeled handcart that the town carrier pushed around Leh.

Now taxi jeeps are common. The queen has a jeep with a fixed metal roof and lace curtains, abbots from some of the grander monasteries have jeeps. The boy behind the counter at the Pamposh Hotel has the remains of a Hero bike. It still goes. When trade is slack, he leaps the counter, bounds across the footpath and the ditch that separate the Pamposh from the street, grabs the bike and does wheelies. Grave shopkeepers look affronted: he is bringing down the tone of the bazaar. But it is impossible that he will do so for long. Every time a customer enters the Pamposh he races back to work, lets the bike fall on the paving stones and performs a flying leap into the teastall.

The boy's Hero is the standard bike of India, big and heavy and built for a staid procession. But it cannot for long survive his treatment. Not that I would ever say a word against the strength of a Hero. No owner has ever complained that these days they don't put the same stuff into them. They do. I know, because the camp carpenter owns one and he lets me borrow it between 5 a.m. and 7 a.m. when castles, monasteries and colonies of chortens are at their crispest for photography. It is a bastard of a thing to ride, though — heavy, clunky, clumsy. But it does cover ground even though one pedal is lost.

Dorjee Gyaltsen has never ridden a bike. But, he says, he will quickly learn the knack. Once I have assembled it for him. He turns spaniel eyes upon me: surely the great, kind, generous and intelligent Ronner-la will not refuse to put the bike together?

I decide to take advantage of him. Okay. I'll do it. Provided I can have the first ride. I'll give it a test run into Leh. He nearly collapses in gratitude. We toast the success of the enterprise.

Getting the bike together turns out to be no trouble. Now that there is no Sonam Dakpa to keep up with, my nightly preparation can be half-hearted or skipped altogether. And I have borrowed *War and Peace* from the Choglamsar Monastery library, such an exciting novel that, for greater

180

speed of reading, I have bought an oil lamp instead of relying on candles. So now I have spare time and light enough to put a bike together. Between dinner and bedtime the three parcels begin to look like a bike. Next day the complete and perfect machine leans against the wall of my cell. Dorjee Gyaltsen will be intoxicated by its flashy modernity.

It is a copy of a bicycle I used to know well. Above my bed in the 1940s hung a sly propaganda photograph showing the English king crossing Windsor Great Park astride a Rudge Sports. He was in a suit and tie but wore no bike-clips because the Rudge was the gentleman's bike, with a guard covering the chain so that its riders had no need to wear

Prayerwheels set in walls: another chance for
a good reincarnation.

181

bike-clips or to push their pants into their socks like greengrocers or bank clerks. In a gig beside the king rode his queen and their girls, nicely hatted and hand-folded, and all of them giving off a subtle and patriotic message: 'Look at all of us, saving benzine like billy-oh.'

His Majesty's Rudge would have had three-ratio Sturmey-Archer gears in the rear hub. Dorjee Gyaltsen's Hero Sports lacks this refinement. So my dashing zoom into town turns into a trudge when the road rises near the All-India Radio mast. But soon the road is level again and the spokes twinkle as I glide past a tract of new houses opposite the desert golf course that the Indian army has laid out, not to use, only to win an entry — highest golf course in the world — in *The Guinness Book of Records*.

Then follows a second push as the road climbs to the bus station on the edge of town. But now comes my triumphal entry. The right leg swings over the saddle and coolly I swoop into the main bazaar and prop the Hero Sports against the kerbing outside the spice merchant's stall. How I glow and strut! For months I have come into Leh each week to do my shopping. Bit by bit the stallholders and I have grown to recognise one another. But only at the shop I call Fortnum and Masons, where two Hindus sell superior cloth, condoms and tinned tuna, has any friendliness developed.

Now, with the Hero Sports looking as glorious as a new Ferrari, stallholders lollop, grinning, towards me. I might be a gold medal winner returning from the Olympics, so eager are they to be with me. They shake hands and pat my shoulder. Then, coyly, they sidle away to stand a respectful pace back from the Hero Sports. One leans forward and gently fondles a mudguard. But someone slaps the fondler's hand and he stands back, abashed by his own impertinence.

This is the only time I ever ride Dorjee Gyaltsen's Hero Sports. But my one ride into town transforms my standing in Leh. Now there is always a wave and a grin from each stallholder in the bazaar.

twenty

Today, as well as wasting hours making the teachers' tea and tidying up after them, Thubke Chophal has been delivering a memo from the headmaster. So precious is paper that the memo comes on a slip of paper no more than five centimetres deep, sliced from a full sheet so that one piece of paper can be made to perform several tasks.

I am still so irresponsible and extravagant that I take the memo from Thubke Chophal, read it and drop it into my desk drawer. Thubke Chophal mimes a correction: I must initial the back of the memo and return it to him so that he can take the one slip of paper around the school.

The memo announces the dates of end-of-year exams and the days when marking must be completed; 28 November is the day for me to report to the headmaster which children from class VIA have passed in maths and which have failed. The term — the year — will end on 3 December. Then, on 4 December, the camp truck will take the first load of children back to Jhun Thang. So 4 December is the day I am free to leave.

Not until I am cooking dinner does the memo hit me. It is my death sentence.

I came here mainly because I had become enchanted with Ladakh — so in love with the people, the rocks and the dust that I had to keep on returning. It was becoming an expensive addiction, and I hoped that, if I overdosed on a school year at Choglamsar, I might return home so hating

Ladakh and so glad to be back that I could think myself cured. But, no, I am uncured. Ladakh has bitten into my brain and is lodged there. When I go home, I shall go into exile.

I force myself to think of the advantages of being home. I can think of only one: flush lavatories.

Yet there is no way of staying, even though rent from my house would keep me in luxury here. So I could manage forever. But, apart from private joys and satisfactions, my year as a volunteer had really had only one result — it has kept a Tibetan teacher out of paid work. Go I must. And every morning I wake to a stabbing thought: one day less of my chosen life.

To console myself, and to drive the stab deeper, I spend Sundays revisiting favourite places. Sabu comes first.

The farmhouse nearest to Choglamsar has a violent, unchained guard dog, so I have learned to swing wide from the track and perform an arcing rock-scramble that now leads me towards a column of chaff rising from within a circle of new-bought flags which ring a threshing floor. In the centre of the circle stands Ex-Deputy Superintendent P.T. Wangyal. I know his name and rank and I know he lives in the big house nearby. A high wall surrounds it and at the highest point of the arched gateway is a sign:

P.T. WANGYAL

EX-DTY SUP POL

In his hands he holds a willow pitchfork — willow handle, willow prongs — with which he is winnowing his barley. In the middle of his threshing floor stands a post to which, yesterday and the day before, he tethered a string of donkeys and dzos and drove them round and round on top of a pile of barley sickled from his fields and carried to the threshing floor on the backs of donkeys. The circling hooves trampled the grain from the ears of barley. Now it is his job to toss the stalks high and let the wind move chaff and stalks sideways while the grains fall straight.

Ex-Deputy Superintendent Wangyal is a slight, upright man with a face entirely free of wrinkles. He retired seven years ago, so he may be sixty-seven. Easily, rhythmically, he works his way downwind to clear the threshing floor of straw and chaff. Upwind of him, a servant girl scoops grains in a pan and tosses them high to clear the last dust and chaff, with which the obliging wind coats Mr Wangyal's face, gown and hands.

He notices me and comes over, blinking away his dressing of dust, to welcome me to Sabu. I tell him how much I enjoy visiting his village. He says he already knows that. He has seen me often. So he made certain enquires — here is the policeman in him talking — and ascertained that I am a respectable citizen who may be allowed to stray a few hundred metres over the line foreigners are not supposed to cross.

I close my eyes and lower my head to acknowledge his indulgence.

He explains, and I think it is with pride, why, in his own life, he also is breaking all the rules. At his age he ought no longer to be occupying the family farmhouse. Instead he should have been eased out into the small dowerhouse, where he could devote his time to being old and feeble while a more vigorous daughter or son ran the farm and assigned harmless little tasks to him.

But he sent his sons to university. One is a civil engineer, the other a doctor. So they have no wish to farm the family land. Nor do his two daughters. They are also educated and have office jobs. This leaves him free to farm. 'I harvest,' he says in a sentence that sounds rehearsed, 'I harvest contentment.'

Mr Wangyal gives the servant girl a command and she goes inside the high wall around the house. While we await her return I ask why he is flying flags on poles around the threshing floor. He looks shrewdly at me as if to let me know that he has seen the real meaning underneath my words: Are those flags some stupid heathen device to keep bad spirits away? 'No,' he answers. 'They are to scare away the birds.'

The servant returns and hands Mr Wangyal a tray of apples. 'My own fruit,' he says and offers them to me: a gift which signals that he still has work to do and that I have his blessing to walk a little further towards the distant line where India and China are still conducting their carefully measured and limited warfare.

Presently, he and the girl are back at their own version of a harvest song. They use a gasping whistle to keep in time with each other, moving scoop and pitchfork to the same beat.

Other Sabu harvesters use other work songs. On a threshing floor where tethered beasts are working in unison, a girl follows with a withy, calling in encouragement, 'Wallu-ballu, wallu-ballu.' But, on another floor, the animals are stroppy and will not keep together. The girl in charge breaks off the encouraging and contented 'Wallu-ballu' song and soars into a screeching 'Yi-yi, yi-yi,' which she reinforces with lashes across the beasts' rumps. This settles them into steady work. So she stops her thrashing and switches to a warning 'Pish-pish, pish-pish', to remind them

The Red Monastery towers above King Senge Namgyal's palace.

their behaviour is being watched. They plod steadily and she encourages continuing good behaviour with a soothing string of 'Wallu-ballu, wallu-ballu'.

Through autumn work and autumn song I walk, then turn right into a side valley, where I drop into the palace for lunch, a ruined palace on a crag. Sitting on a stone floor amid teetery walls, I survey the little dukedom. I watch haystacks walking from fields to threshing floors, donkey hooves clip-clopping underneath the golden loads. I hear work chants, I feel Wangyal apple juice jet around my mouth. The palace coos with the contentment of pigeons bloated from autumn gorging and now dozing on sills and ledges.

From high above a hawk comes down the ridge. The pigeons turn crazy. In roofless towers they clatter their wings and launch themselves into enemy airspace, sometimes bunching beneath the raider like a shoal of threatened fish, sometimes spreading to fill as much sky as one pair of eyes can see.

Insolently at ease, the hawk hangs above them, holding the air with unmoving wings. If he wishes, he can grab any bird he fancies and tear it apart for lunch. But today he is only checking that he still has a palaceful of food to see him through the winter — and ample pigeons which, turned gormless by his approach, can be relied on to fly upwards and present themselves for his choice instead of trying to hide.

For a while he circles the palace, eyes his supplies and then, having completed his larder census, shrugs a shoulder, banks to starboard and heads for higher slopes. As his silhouette shrinks the wing-clatter of fear fades, the palace refills with pigeons, still too unsettled to coo, and in the new silence I hear from all over Sabu the chants that ease the harvest work.

twenty-one

Igo to the headmaster to tell him I am starting extra maths tuition again. He nods. When I walk away from his office I curse myself for a coward.

Of course I had to let him know. It's a school rule that pupils are not to be in teachers' cells without the headmaster's permission. But really I was driven to his office by the memory of the discipline master's visit at the end of last term when his dark shape filled the doorway and the shadow of dread fell over the children. So, in going to the headmaster, I am at heart looking for borrowed authority to use as a defence if the discipline master calls again. That's why I curse myself — for needing the headmaster's support to give me backbone.

Anyway, the first extra maths session is crowded with guilty slackers who, like sinners filled with fear by some hellfire preacher, want a quick burst of salvation before sliding back into their old ways. With the slackers come all the diligent pupils who are going to pass anyway. Among them is Rigpa Dorjee, the stunted boy who used to hide in the back row among all the muscular dunces.

When Sonam Dakpa was expelled I managed to winkle Rigpa Dorjee out of the back row and get him to sit in Sonam Dakpa's place. Hiding his face, blushing and giggling, he moved his books and crouched behind them with downcast face and averted eyes. But, once his shyness faded, I found it easier to give him attention. Now he glows with achievement.

The morning I announce extra maths I ask Dawa Metok and Dorjee Namgyal to stay behind at morning break. This sets off a great stir: grins, nudges, head-turning, tittering and talk. When calm returns, I decide that I will make a great performance out of what I am going to tell Dawa Metok and Dorjee Namgyal. Other teachers take their classes while sitting behind their desks. But I teach on my feet. This time, though, I prepare myself for Dawa Metok and Dorjee Namgyal by moving to my chair, using this strange posture to create occasion and authority.

When the bell for playtime rings, I rest my forearms on my desk and watch the other students dawdling out, reluctant to miss the coming confrontation. With exaggerated gravity, I rise and follow the departing children to give them a hurry-up. Outside, I stand on the concrete platform and, my face frozen, will them to be off. They fade into the mob of playtime pupils. I return to my seat, extend my arm in the direction of Dawa Metok and Dorjee Namgyal and give them the Tibetan beckoning sign.

'Dawa Metok,' I say when they are standing before me. 'Dorjee Namgyal' — and let a small silence fall and extend itself.

When they are looking sufficiently worried I speak again. 'If you want to come to extra maths I'll be glad to have you. But this time you must bring your books with you. Exercise books. Textbooks. I don't mind. But books. You must at least look as if you're there to work. Understand?'

They look relieved that this is all I have to say. But no brightening comes to their eyes, no smile to show they have penetrated my Oriental indirectness. I try to make myself more scrutable. 'I'm happy that you two enjoy being together. But you must look as if you're there to work. Otherwise the discipline master . . .'

But my voice tails off. I cannot bring myself to betray my side of the teachers-versus-pupils divide. So, letting the chance to warn them slip, I stand. 'Okay. Just remember. Bring books.'

Together we walk into the open, together we emerge on to the platform, together we advertise some sort of plotting. Further along the platform the other teachers are sitting in the sun having morning tea. Heads lift and turn to look at us. Dawa Metok and Dorjee Namgyal go down the steps into the quad. I join the teachers.

The only empty seat is beside the discipline master. I turn to give him a nod. But as soon as my head swings towards him, his swings away. He will not let our eyes meet.

Dawa Metok and Dorjee Namgyal bring their books. And bring their books. Then, on day three, they fail to bring their books. That is the day the discipline master calls.

He strides through the doorway, picks his way over cross-legged children and stares down at Dawa Metok and Dorjee Namgyal. He asks nothing, says nothing. Before he came, they were sitting close together whispering. Dorjee Namgyal had begun a series of urging movements, grinning and nudging her. Under the discipline master's gaze they flick apart and stare up at his silence. Briefly they manage to retain expressions of questioning innocence, then Dawa Metok begins to look around the floor.

She shoves the girl in front of her, lifts a fold in the girl's skirt and stares under it. She turns around and examines the floor behind her. She raises her head again and offers the discipline master a puzzled expression, as if only moments ago her books had been lying beside her — and now what can have happened to them?

Dorjee Namgyal, though, is too assured to try any pretence. This has been a good term for him. He put on a visible spurt of confidence after the school sports. Throughout the day he kept winning so many events that he had to develop a technique for accepting the cheers of his fellow pupils. He would face the crowd, head drooped, back bowed, face calm but with an expression of impatience as if all the claps were mosquitoes that must be put up with. Throughout the term his assurance has continued to develop so that today, when the discipline master stares down at him, he has moved past Dawa Metok's need to mime the lie that her books must have disappeared.

Instead he looks up frankly at the discipline master, grins, makes a slight shrug and spreads apart his upward-turning palms. This is man talk meaning: 'She's got the hots for me. You know the score. Don't try to tell me you'd pass up your chances.'

The discipline master quits the room. Neither in entering nor in leaving has he once faced me. I am too stung by this contempt to see what Dorjee Namgyal does next but, on hearing a cry from Rigpa Dorjee, I swing my eyes back from the retreating figure of the discipline master.

Dorjee Namgyal is holding Rigpa Dorjee by his hair. Rigpa Dorjee's face is in pain. Dorjee Namgyal shouts at him in English (for my benefit?), 'You bloody told him, you bloody told him, you bloody told him!' With every shout he yanks at Rigpa Dorjee's hair. Dawa Metok tries to unclasp Dorjee Namgyal's hand and shouts in Tibetan, 'He is too small, Let go.'

I stand and try to get through the seated children. Dorjee Namgyal notices me, gives one great wrench at Rigpa Dorjee's hair and lets go. Freed, Rigpa Dorjee rockets up and out the door. But Dorjee Namgyal follows. So the little boy has no chance. He must be in the same panic as an animal being driven into a net by dogs and armed men, because rather than turning left or right into open space he runs straight at the rear wall of the hospital.

Dawa Metok beats me to the door of my cell. Over her head I see Dorjee Namgyal land a punch. Rigpa Dorjee falls. Dorjee Namgyal gets in a kick. Rigpa Dorjee writhes. Dawa Metok grabs Dorjee Namgyal by the shoulders and tries to pull him back from Rigpa Dorjee. 'Stop, stop! He is too small.' She twists her body to get in between Dorjee Namgyal and Rigpa Dorjee's fallen figure. She pushes Dorjee Namgyal away from the smaller boy and calls into his face, 'Go away. Go away. Now.' He refuses. She glares: 'Go away. Go away.'

Pam and Karoly come running. Now heavily outnumbered, Dorjee Namgyal takes one step back. In seconds he has fallen from school hero to pariah and does not know the movements for the transformation. I go up to him: 'Just piss off.'

He stands fast.

Then I remember a tabu Tibetan word. It sounds like 'pahtyuk' and when I shout it in his face shock and shame cover Dorjee Namgyal's expression. He begins to back off, torn between the dignity of walking away at his own pace and of running in disgrace.

Next morning Dawa Metok moves her place in the classroom. She takes over the desk of one of the sexpot girls who sit curling lips at me from the heat of the window. There Dawa Metok spends the day's maths lesson staring out into the quad, choked with dignity, excluding Dorjee Namgyal from her glance and ignoring all work.

Two days pass. Then on the third day, a Wednesday, the discipline master arrives in the quad when the children are still only halfway through morning chants.

We must by then have had at least a month without any of his thrashings up on the punishment block. When he arrives I think I feel a flicker of tension pass through the chanting children but, when I look into individual faces for signs of fear, I notice nothing. And I myself have no clue to what the man's arrival can mean. In our rum-and-gossip sessions Dorjee Gyaltsen has come up with no talk of scandals brewing. I stare into Dawa Metok's face and look at Dorjee Namgyal. No fretful movements there, no show of apprehension.

When the chanting ends I am again looking at her when, from the punishment block, comes the shout: 'Dawa Metok!' Her body judders in the way that a rabbit's does when a bullet strikes. Automatically her hands clasp together and rush to cover her mouth but she makes no other movement until her name is shouted again from the discipline block.

As if bearing a weight, she begins moving foward. She is wearing clunky second-hand work-boots that must have come from some European charity. She is sockless and the boots are too large for her. So feet and boots are a split second out of kilter. A foot lifts. The boot stays still until the ankle moves across the void behind the laces and then makes contact and lifts the boot along. This tiny slip in co-ordination, this bumpkin lack of polish, suddenly injects me with a moment of indifference. Why should I, comfortable foreigner, have any concern for this gauche, plain, clumsy, dusty girl plodding through the crowded quad towards the punishment block?

For that second an iron door clangs. I could stand up, put my hands in my pockets and walk away without wondering what is to happen to her.

Then the second passes. At the foot of the steps she pauses and, with a movement so graceful that it looks rehearsed, she lowers her hands, lifts and spreads the hem of her gown and, now freed of the fear of tripping, lifts her head and climbs. Up on the block she keeps her gaze steadily level and forward. Like a queen on the scaffold, she ignores the discipline master. She moves to the edge of the block, where slowly she brings her hands together in front of her and calmly looks out above and beyond the hushed mass of children.

The voice of the discipline master crumples this scene of calm and courage. He calls 'Dorjee Namgyal!' and sends a shock through the quad. Dorjee Namgyal the sports hero? Dorjee Namgyal the heart throb? Can even he be beaten and shamed up on the punishment block?

Head up and trying to force back the start of a smile, he strides easily through the press of children. With his trademark light, quick movements, he leaps on to the block and stands beside and close to Dawa Metok. She gives him an affronted glare which, in full public view, forces him to make a reluctant sideways step away from her.

Now the discipline master begins to address the assembly and, as he speaks, Dawa Metok and Dorjee Namgyal slide into the penitents' posture: backs bowed, heads lowered, arms out sideways but not yet into the total abasement of begging for mercy by sticking out their tongues and scraping fingers forward across the skull.

'Something very serious, something shaming, has happened,' says the discipline master. He has no English. My Tibetan is still rudimentary. But I am getting the drift, which I confirm later when Dorjee Gyaltsen and I are sitting with our sundowners.

'Two trusted pupils have been found guilty of having a love affair,' says the discipline master. 'They have been exchanging love letters. I know because during the school holidays I found the letters in their tin trunks. The guilty pupils are Dorjee Namgyal and Dawa Metok, and it is beyond me to tell you which of them is the greater sinner.

'You all remember the start of the year when our director called the whole school together in the camp assembly hall. You remember that Dorjee Gyaltsen was one of the five fathers. We had to expel a house mother for lewd behaviour, and we had to stop the pocket money of the five boys she had lain with.

'The other four boys accepted their punishment. For their behaviour with the house mother they lost merit. By accepting their punishment they rebuilt merit. But not Dorjee Namgyal. He refused to accept the loss of spending money. Instead he wheedled money out of Dawa Metok. Here is the letter asking her for money. Here also is the letter thanking her for money.

'After that he wrote indecent letters to Dawa Metok. But at exactly the time he was making suggestions to Dawa Metok he was also asking another girl — a second girl! — for money. She rejected him. Otherwise she would be standing here today. Otherwise you would today see on this platform alongside Dorjee Namgyal two girls who were willing to pay for Dorjee Namgyal's attention.'

To Dawa Metok, mention of another girl comes as a lash. The tension sags from her knees and her back. Her hands move from the ritual outspread posture of shame and rush to her eyes. She begins rhythmic sobbing. Briefly Dorjee Namgyal gives her a glance of curiosity.

'Dawa Metok,' announces the discipline master, 'gave Dorjee Namgyal five rupees.'

In my own money five rupees is sixty cents — such a fortune to children here that the assembled children gasp.

'Yes, five rupees. Five rupees. She spends five rupees to buy a boy's attention. This was shameless. But consider her circumstances and you will see it was not only shameless. It was evil. Heartless.

'Last year Dawa Metok's mother died. Her mother's soul is still in Bardo awaiting rebirth. If Dawa Metok had any real love for her mother, if she had any proper concern for her mother's next incarnation, she would have taken those five rupees to the monastery for prayers for her mother's next body. That is what any decent child would do. Instead she gave it to a boy to buy his favour.'

At the mention of her dead mother, Dawa Metok's steady sobbing shifts to terrible spasms. Her head lolls sideways. Her face is twisted. She makes shuddering moans. She looks as if she will lose all control and fall from the punishment block.

The discipline master falls silent. He needs to say no more. The sight and the sound of her agony become sermon enough. Slowly Dawa Metok's cries ebb. Her shaking loses its violence. The heartbreak rhythm of her sobbing returns.

The discipline master turns to his verdict. 'No behaviour has ever given me such worry over proper punishment.' He lets his voice fall. He stretches out our ache of waiting to hear his decision. 'But now I have decided. These two lovebirds would do anything to be together. So I am going to rope them together.

'Tied to one another by cords around the ankles, they will work for two days up in the desert behind the school. There they will fill sacks with sand. Then, every time two sacks are filled, they will each hoist a loaded sack on to their backs. They will bring them down to a table in the quad. On the table will be a book. And for every sack of sand they bring they will each write in the book: 'I have sinned.'

'For two days from your classrooms you other children will watch Dawa Metok and Dorjee Namgyal enter the quad bent under the weight of their own evil. And you will see them writing in the book that they have sinned. For two days you will watch their public shaming and, as you watch, you will decide in your own hearts that the path of sin is not the path that you will take.'

From a pocket, the discipline master withdraws a length of cord and mockingly swings it through the air. 'From your classrooms you will watch our lovebirds pick up their loads again and lug them down to the school lavatories, where they will make a great pile of sand — sand enough to last the lavatory monitors a year. Sand carrying is a lowly task for people who place themselves above the rules of this school — a twice-lowly task because the sand will be used to scatter over all your droppings.'

This must have been a sharper jibe than I could understand. The children in the quad laughed jeeringly. Dorjee Namgyal reared up his head and looked wildly about.

The discipline master fell to one knee and roped Dawa Metok and Dorjee Namgyal together. Then, rising, he pointed to the instruments of punishment. 'There are your shovels. There are your sacks. Walk across the quad. Pick up your sacks and shovels. For two days let us hear nothing but silence from you. And for two days you shall feel nothing but the weight and pain of your own transgressions.'

twenty-two

For two days I watch Dawa Metok and Dorjee Namgyal enter the quad, let their sacks slide to the ground, step forward to the table, write 'I have sinned', lift their sacks and stumble down to the lavatories.

For two days Dawa Metok adds to her labours by trying to keep as far from Dorjee Namgyal as the cord around their ankles will allow. For two days her effort forces both to stumble every time the cord goes taut. And for two days Dawa Metok seems to weep without cease. At the end of each day she has a runnel of tears cutting a clear pathway through the powdering of dust on her face.

On the day after their punishment, she is standing alone in the quad looking abandoned. Chanting is over. The school bell is about to start the day. She is beside the concrete platform that runs along the classrooms and she is leaning against it as if to blot up all the warmth the autumn sun can provide. As soon as I spot her I go up and ask, 'How are you feeling after all that?'

She manages to get a smile started but before it is going properly her eyes become unfocused. Her knees give way. She slides down the concrete wall and lies in a crumple.

Two of the biggest girls are watching. I summon them. Dawa Metok has turned into deadweight but I manage to lift her and to get each of her arms hooked around the necks of the other girls. Slowly (Christ! Why are they such oxen?) they grasp the idea of anchoring her in place by grasping her wrists. When they are holding her securely, I tell them to take Dawa Metok to the hospital.

The bell rings. The rest of us troop indoors. The girls are quickly back.

'You got Dawa Metok to hospital?'

'Yes, sir.'

'Yes, sir.'

At mid-morning break I walk over to the hospital. Pam, the false rimpoche's wife, the Canadian nurse and Karoly are sitting on the steps soaking sun.

'How's Dawa Metok?'

Blank stares.

'Dawa Metok. The girl I sent over earlier.'

No girls today. Only two skiving boys.

I stare back at the school. Two hundred metres of dust and rock. Nowhere for those girls to have hidden a body — nowhere except maybe the row of willows that grow along the edge of the overflow from the water pipe in front of my cell. I walk the line of trees. No. No Dawa Metok dumped under the branches. Now I notice the invisible building. The abandoned superloo.

In the space of two years the superloo has become an historic monument completely ignored and politely unnoticed. The story behind it is that a Miss Rockefeller visited the refugee camp and asked, 'Where's the bathroom?' Discreetly she was ushered into one of the camp lavatories. Within seconds, pale and gagging, she rushed back into the open air and instead went behind a large boulder.

And no wonder. The mud-brick lavatories are built out over gullies and slopes. Inside each building lies one long compartment that can take ten or a dozen people at a time. Each compartment is floored with timber over which sand is tossed. Down the centre of each compartment runs a gap in the floor across which users are supposed to crouch. Adults can comfortably manage to straddle the slits and, while they are crouched, they are able to entertain themselves by looking down and seeing sparrows and camp dogs entering the dung chamber below them to forage for partly digested scraps that may turn out to be edible. But to the smallest children the slit in the floor is alarmingly wide. Rather than risk falling through it, they crouch against the wall, as far from the slit as they can manage, and leave their droppings on the floor.

Miss Rockefeller, accustomed to wealth and trained for action, came to an instant decision while squatting behind her giant boulder. She would stay in the camp's guest apartment and remain there until, at her own expense and under her direction, builders had completed less vile lavatories. She designed some along the lines of the raised benches pierced with bum-sized holes that ancient Romans used. Underneath would run a stone-walled canal to carry running water from the pipe near my cell.

The building was completed. The water was diverted. Miss Rockefeller, the camp director, the notables of Choglamsar village assembled for the opening. A muttering started and spread. People pointed at the way the water flowed out of the Rockefeller lavatory. People started either to titter or to look embarrassed. They walked beside the water flowing from the lavatory and saw what would happen if ever the superloo was used. An open sewer of stinking effluent would flow over the ground, would run past the school, past the camp office, through the staff housing block, over the road and into Choglamsar village itself.

Tactfully, the massed dignitaries kept their eyes away from Miss Rockefeller and began to walk from the scene of the grand opening that now would never happen. Miss Rockefeller, too, melted away. When people went to the guest apartment to look for her, there were Kleenex tissues on the floor and bits of the casual detritus of the rich but no luggage and no Miss Rockefeller. She had faded away just like her dream of bringing sanitation to her pet Tibetans.

But Dawa Metok, where is she?

Through the deserted superloo I go, wrenching open the doors of each compartment. Dawa Metok lies in the last, dumped there to die. I lift her body's unresponsive weight and drape her around my neck like a shawl.

On the hospital steps the others jump at the sight of my staggering approach. They lead me to the nearest bed. I ease Dawa Metok on to it. She lies motionless. Karoly presses his stethoscope to her chest. He makes no movement. Then he puts out a hand for silence. He closes his eyes and raises his head. We all stop breathing.

Afterwards I tell Pam and Karoly about the sandbagging. Could that have caused it? They shake their heads. They had noticed Dawa Metok and Dorjee Namgyal stumbling down from behind the hospital and had got the false rimpoche's wife to find out what was going on. Then, like doctors watching a boxing bout, they had gone over to have a word with the two and make sure they were not being harmed. No damage was being done. So, like me, they held back from interfering.

'What could you do?' asks Pam. 'We're just the foreigners here. Every now and then we'd take a dekko and check there was no sign of, you know, collapse. If things had got awful, we would've stepped in. But we're only the visitors. We're not running the show.'

Dawa Metok is lying in a room of her own just inside the entrance, away from the main ward. Her heartbeat is slight and slow. She is only just breathing.

The hospital has virtually no equipment, no laboratory. It gets a catch-as-catch-can collection of drugs from European charities. So there are gaps in what Pam and Karoly would like to have and an oversupply of stuff they expect never to need. They are convinced Dawa Metok's illness has nothing to do with the sandbag-humping. It's almost certainly some sort of infection. But what infection?

They shrug. Already Pam and Karoly have clicked into the tiny medical mafia of Leh. They have been to the civil hospital to say their how-do-you-dos and have visited the military hospital. Now they plan to take samples and see if they can use the civil hospital lab to do some tests. But they are not overconfident.

'You wouldn't bloody believe it,' says Pam. 'The civil hospital's got bugger-all gear. Even the microscope's an old brass thing that schoolkids would laugh at.'

At the military hospital they had no time to inspect the place because, according to Pam, the major in charge and Karoly spent all their time talking about wars. But she expects it will have all the latest gear — 'with bells and bloody whistles. Those buggers never stint themselves.' Karoly scowls. At home he is a major in the territorial army, and at my rum sessions I have heard him trying to explain to Dorjee Gyaltsen why everybody must be on the alert, ready to fight when the Indonesians invade.

Dawa Metok's face has turned the same ivory shade as Sonam Dakpa's. Days come and go. She lies still, faintly breathing. Every two hours the nurses roll her over. 'We mustn't get bedsores, must we?' says the Canadian. But Dawa Metok makes no reply. She is still comatose.

Pam and Karoly grow impatient with my visits to the hospital. Why do I sit on a chair staring at her face? She is going to come right, they say. Every day her heartbeat and her breathing are getting better. And they have worked out what is wrong with her. It's a kidney infection. The civil hospital helped with the diagnosis and the major at the military hospital slipped Karoly some medicine — 'stuff-all, actually,' says Pam. 'But I suppose we can't complain. You know what the army's like: forms in triplicate and court-martials if they can't account for every glass of water.'

There is at least one reason why I keep looking in to see Dawa Metok: because no one else does. No teachers. No one from the camp office. Her father, just down the road at the Indo-Tibetan Border Police barracks, has not been told, nor her brother, the little sacristan in the palace chapel.

Dorjee Gyaltsen — even Dorjee Gyaltsen, who wants to grow out of being Tibetan — is puzzled and uneasy. My visits, he says, 'are very bad luck. And it was wrong thing to take her to hospital.' When I found her crumpled in the Rockefeller lavatories the proper procedure would have been to consult a lama. The usual cause of any sickness, says Dorjee Gyaltsen, is a curse. The lama could have undone the curse and she would have got well again. After that, the lama would have got me to buy a sheep and tie a red ribbon around its neck. The ribbon would show that the sheep had been consecrated. And that would save it from slaughter.

So my buying it would save a life. And the merit for saving a life would have been banked not in my own but in Dawa Metok's good-deeds account. So she would be in credit, which would act as a future protection for her. In addition, the lama could give her a new name and the camp could give her new clothes — new name, new clothes, new person. And because she would then have been made a new person, the curse that had been placed on the former Dawa Metok would have nowhere to go. It would wander homeless. That would be extra protection. But automatically that protection would wear away if she had visitors.

Dorjee Gyaltsen is sorry to have to say this, but my visits are making her worse. In a well-conducted household, if someone became ill, the family would keep a very smoky fire burning by the courtyard entrance. This would be a sign of illness and everybody would respect it by staying away. But in case ignorant people ignored the message of the fire, a lama would sell the family blessed incense to keep beside the sickbed if visitors came, because they would inevitably bring painful and troublesome spirits with them.

Then the family would light the incense and blow the smoke from it into the patient's face until he coughed up evil spirits. The family would then take the remains of the incense outdoors. The coughed-up spirits would accompany the incense, which would now be thrown away and spat on. This would destroy the spirits. Healing would continue.

Dorjee Gyaltsen tries to comfort me: 'It is not your blaming. How could you know? But that false rimpoche, his wife she should have told the new doctors.'

twenty-three

Outside the hospital and beyond the camp walls, winter falls like a whip. The harvest is in, poured by the panful into striped handwoven goat-hair sacks and lugged into the granary of every house.

At school, though, we refuse to take shelter. It is too cold to go indoors. As the northern end of the earth's axis tips away from the pale sun, the classrooms turn into ice chambers. And this is a blessing. The fifty children who, all summer, elbowed, pinched and kicked one another because they were jammed too tightly in their classroom, now move out into the quad for lessons in the sunlight, cross-legged on the tarseal, their bottoms insulated by cushions of layered exercise books.

The sun's retreat imposes a new etiquette: children must sit well apart because if a neighbour's shadow falls, say, on a hand, the hand instantly feels amputated — warm, alive and comfortable up to the shadowline, but cold and dead within the shade. So the year's death brings strange peace, each child at ease in ample space of its own, too far apart to punch or kick and now fired by the urgency of exams.

But for me no peace comes, only an embarrassing wallow in self-pity. Daily I stare at my wall calendar. I am a prisoner — an innocent prisoner — on death row.

Today I have only nineteen days to go. Then I shall be expelled, forced on to an aeroplane and sent back to the desperate tedium of sitting in an office making marks on bits of paper, of talking into telephones, of fidgeting through meetings, of staring out the window at walls of steel and concrete and mirror-glass, walls so high they steal the sky.

Inside the hospital, thanks to air-conditioning, it is still summer for Dawa Metok. When I was away in the hills the camp carpenters built a false ceiling thirty centimetres or so below the log, twig and mud roof. Into the gap they stuffed an insulating blanket of barley straw. On the south-facing wall of the main ward they knocked out two mud bricks, one just above the floor, the other near the ceiling.

Around these holes they brushed black paint over a large swathe of

Outside the old people's temple at the refugee camp.

outer wall, and on to the blackened wall they built a giant glazed picture-frame, the upper cross-member of which was hinged. Next they went to the shaded northern wall of the ward and took out a third brick close to the floor and fitted the gap with a trapdoor. A second trapdoor was built to block or open the upper gap in the sunny wall.

The picture-frame must have been four metres long and two metres high, and all through the forty-degree summer the sun's heat beating on the blackened wall was trapped behind the glass of the frame — or it would have been trapped if the hinged upper part of the frame had not been opened. So the heated air disappeared through the opening, and as it went up into the sky its place was taken by cooler air lying on the floor of the ward. In turn the cooler air's disappearance meant that even colder air was sucked into the ward from the pool of shade lying outside the northern wall. As summer slid into winter, the trapdoor high in the

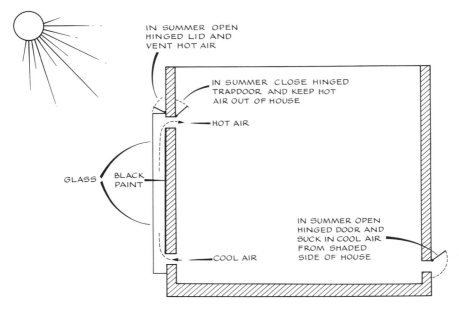

The air-conditioning wall in the hospital.

southern wall was opened and the hinged part of the picture-frame was closed.

Now, in winter, the endless sun still beats upon the black wall and still heats the air inside the picture-frame. But the heat, instead of being vented and wasted on the outer air, pours like a furnace blast into the ward and, as it leaves its hothouse, it draws after it a gulp of floor-level air, which enters a daylong current of constantly warmer air circulating through the heater, into the ward and back into the heater.

Dawa Metok has been moved from her back room and into the subtropics of the main ward. She is the only patient. She is no longer in a coma. Sometimes she opens her eyes, sometimes she stares at the wall.

At lunchtime and after school I visit her and bring oranges from the Kashmiri girl's stall opposite the camp entrance. Dawa Metok is too feeble and apathetic to pick up segments of orange and slip them into her mouth. So, if her eyes are open when I visit, I squeeze the halves and put the cup to her lips. Sometimes she manages all the juice, sometimes the effort is too great and she falls back after the first sip.

The oranges and the visits cannot last much longer. The Kashmiri girl says trucks cannot get over Zoji La any more because of snow. So we are back to being enclosed by impassable roads and trails: no more fruit from India until the thaw.

By then I shall be long gone. I had hoped for one last ride along the two-day switchback road down to Srinagar. But the booking clerk at the bus station laughed: 'My dear sir, you know nothing of Ladakh. Every day we already expect too much snow. Yet you want a seat in one fortnight. By then no buses can run.' So I am booked to fly out. I, who cannot bear to leave, am being forced to use this drabbest way of being ejected.

Everyone is trying to be kind. Even classes which I have never taught invite me to farewell afternoon teas. Each farewell is nearly identical. For the occasion children are driven back into their frozen classrooms. They remove desks and line the walls with chairs. In front of two seats of honour stands a table covered with a cloth on which are placed two cups of tea and a plate of biscuits. The class teacher and I enter the room. The children stand. The teacher and I sit. The children sit. The teacher and I sip. We each nibble on a biscuit and wonder what to talk about. The children urge us to eat more. We decline. Now the plate is passed around. The teacher and I watch the children eat and still we wonder what to say. The children swallow the crumbs and sing in my honour. They present a painted scroll or an address of thanks.

The teacher and I leave first. Outside we stand saying thank you and goodbye. When the children come out I wave goodbye to them. They freeze and put their hands to their mouths, uncertain whether waving back would undermine the great dignity of the occasion. I walk home, wishing I could be weeping with gratitude for kindness rather than hating this latest reminder that I must go.

One day, returning from yet another farewell, I see Lobsang Tensing and Jigme Kunga standing outside my door with a parcel. Dorjee Gyaltsen has warned me that they have a present to give me and, after my collapse of proper manners by visiting Dawa Metok, he has impressed on me the necessity to behave correctly. I must hesitate to inspect the parcel. The director and Kunga La will respond by urging me to look inside. When I do look at the gift, I must show no sign of pleasure. That would only advertise greed and attachment to material things. Smiles or thanks would expose a base and shamelessly grasping nature, and that would embarrass the director and Kunga La. They would think they were encouraging improper attitudes.

Inside my cell, the presentation of the gift goes according to predictions. The director hands over the package. With calm indifference I accept it. Kunga La urges me to open it. Inside lies one rolled-up handknotted rug from the camp's own workshop. I unroll it and see a pattern worked in viridian green, orange and gentian: so garish and so crude that I cannot hold back a look of dismay. The director and Kunga La beam with appreciation. I, still po-faced, glow at the thought of how well I have passed the test of good manners. 'Not to forget,' says Kunga La as they

The monastery at Tiksey looks out over the heartland
of Ladakh.

leave. 'Tomorrow morning quite sharp at nine the jeep is taking you.'

Long before the jeep comes I am ready. How could I not be? There is only one backpack to fill. Even the rug, athwart the top of the pack, fits roped down under the upper flap. On the concrete platform outside my cell I stand fretting for the jeep to come and take me quickly. And I worry about Dawa Metok. I have not said goodbye. Nor shall I. But I must duck over to the hospital for one last look. Pale, asleep and imitating death? Or pale, asleep and hinting at recovery?

The answer is a miracle. She is sitting up talking to Pam.

'Ah, sitting up!' I say. (Hospital visitors always have a refreshing and unexpected line of conversation.)

From outside I hear the jeep's engine, I hear the thump of my pack being tossed on its tray. 'Damn, I've got to go,' I say to Pam.

She walks to the door with me. 'Today,' she says, 'this is the first time

I have let myself think she is going to pull through. Of course,' her voice tails off, 'it's still early days.'

I swing around and go back to Dawa Metok. She is lying down again, eyes closed. I bend and touch her cheek. 'See yer,' I say.

Her eyes open. She makes a grin. I stand straight, organise my face, go over to the door and give Pam a peck.

'See yer,' she says.

'Yup,' I reply. 'See yer.'

Then, just like young Carstairs, I get my face in order again — jaws clenched, eyes blinked dry, lips tight, everything under control — and stride to the jeep and hop in. I want to mix in some Bogart with the Carstairs and I try to tell the driver: 'Okay, fella, let's get the hell outa this place.'

But all I can manage is silence.

epilogue

I fly to Delhi, stretch out in a marble bath and watch myself disappear. A confetti of scurf flutters up from all over my body and scums the bathwater: a floating white blanket, a steaming white blanket, the harvest of skin that has gone unwashed all those months.

Months. Good grief, it's December already. Back home, sweating in summer dresses or cotton shorts, the windowdressers will be spraying white drifts of imitation snow deep and crisp and even. They are making plastic fir trees droop under the weight of fake Christmas. They are turning shops' plateglass into ye olde windowpanes, spraying twinkly flakes from cans of glitter until it piles in heaps on imitation ledges. Inside stores, ceaseless tapes play *Jingle Bells White Christmas Mary's Boy Child Little Drummer Boy Silent Night.*

Do I really have to go back to all that tackiness? Can't I, just this once, bypass Rudolph and Santa and all those fat faces shouting about themselves at office parties? Well, can't I?

Yes, I can. My plane ticket lets me go on to Rome and London, then back home through Cairo, Bombay, Bangkok, Tokyo.

After the cheery filth of Ladakh I shall never be able to face grubby hangdog London tarted up in whory tinsel. But the Italians may be more stylish — no fibreglass reindeer across the dome of St Peters. They may even be trying to ignore Christmas until the very last.

So that's fixed. I'll do a Moghul wallow — Old Delhi and Agra —

then Rome and Florence, the antiquities museum in Cairo, an overnight hop to catch the bullet train to Kyoto to let my eyes have a week of fondling temples, palaces and gardens. Calm and polished elegance without one ho-ho-ho or mistletoe hanging over cash registers. Then home for New Year.

But everything goes wrong. I get to Rome and Florence and back to Rome, where I start peeing Guinness. When I walk my gut judders with pain. It's hepatitis.

A doctor at the Institute for Tropical Diseases offers a choice — a hospital bed or an instant dash for the airport. The law requires him to report all hepatitis cases. But if I move instantly I'll beat the no-exit order the Ministry of Health computer will soon be flashing to every airport and border post.

So I run. Two days later, feeble and hazy, I drift into Auckland Hospital and am put in an isolation suite, one great room scrubbed to death, with a shower for me alone and a twinkly porcelain lavatory pan. The nurses apologise. The cleaners are on strike and everything is in a mess. Look! A piece of fluff on the floor. See! Over in the corner.

People who say they are my family arrive hooded, gowned, masked and look at me. Their eyes seem alarmed. I know that in Choglamsar fat and flesh disappeared. Skin grew taut, bones jutted. And now my skin is sicklied over with yellow. I must have that cancer-deathbed look. I don't care. I only want to sleep.

So I drowse and totter. Santa passes unseen, I am allowed home, I start growing brisker. Then a strange voice rings: 'Come to dinner, meet my daughter.'

The daughter is the lost lexicographer. No, she didn't ever get to Ladakh, got sick instead. From Srinagar she made tiny bus-hops towards Delhi. For an hour or two she could stand the movement but then had to get out, crawl into cruddy hotels and lie building up strength for the next bus ride.

Well, meeting the lost lexicographer killed one mystery. But how about

Dawa Metok? Did she survive? I wrote to Pam and Karoly and hoped Pam would reply to say Dawa Metok got better. And I hoped and I hoped. Two months later my letter came back. On the envelope were three new words: 'Gone No Address'.

I thought of writing to Dorjee Gyaltsen or Jigme Kunga. Why not Dawa Metok herself? But time passed. Nothing got done. It all seemed a long way away: another country, another time.

PALACES IN THE SKY